Mr & Mrs. Arthur I Weeks

Dynamics of Christian Discipleship

Copyright, 1962
PATHWAY PRESS
Cleveland, Tennessee

All Rights Reserved
Printed in the United States of America

DYNAMICS OF CHRISTIAN DISCIPLESHIP

An Adventure in Christian Living

BY HOLLIS L. GREEN

PATHWAY PRESS
Cleveland   Tennessee

This book is dedicated to the

TREMONT AVENUE CHURCH OF GOD

*Greenville, South Carolina,
and those faithful followers of
Jesus Christ, with whom
I have worked and worshipped.*

FOREWORD

Couched in choice language that reflects the writer's unique skill of expression, this book depicts man in his quest for the real life found in Christ. He states that "Since the flaming sword barred the gate of Eden, man had traveled a maze of pathways in his search for the tree of life." The author very descriptively pictures the divine daybreak for fallen man which was the coming of Christ, the dayspring from on high, to give light to those in darkness and in the shadow of death, and to guide their feet in the way of peace.

The writer very beautifully points to Christ as "the way, the truth, and the life." However, with strong words and the Holy Scripture as his basis, he lists Christ's demands for true discipleship. He states that a disciple must live the gospel he believes. He further says, "A theology not based on experience and testimony cannot be Christian. Thus each life must manifest the work of the Master Teacher in daily deed and devotion."

Hollis L. Green, a native of Tennessee, has been active in the Church of God since childhood. He was educated in the public schools of Chattanooga and furthered his education at Beckley College (West Virginia) and the University of Cincinnati. He has served as evangelist, new field worker, pastor, assistant pastor, director of Christian education, State Sunday School and Youth Director and as a member of State and National Youth Boards. He is an ordained minister in the Church of God.

As a teen-age youth leader, he became interested in the work of Christian education and has participated widely in the youth and Sunday School activities of the church. He served with distinction as a state director for six years, and three years as assistant pastor of the denomination's largest church. In addition to his work within the church, he has served as a representative of the National Sunday School Association and was for five years a member of the General Council of that organization.

His keen interest in Christian journalism dates back to high school and college papers. His generous contribution to the church in this field includes numerous articles and brochures, youth program material, a youth-camp study course and a work on vocational guidance. He believes that Christian journalism is a vital part of his ministry.

Cecil B. Knight
National Director, Sunday School and
Youth Department of the Church of God

STUDY COURSE FOR SUNDAY SCHOOL AND YOUTH WORKERS

The revised Workers' Training Course program of the Church of God includes seven curriculum classifications:

I GENERAL (100 series)

II BIBLE (200 series)

III CHURCH DOCTRINE (300 series)

IV CHRISTIAN LIVING (400 series)

V EVANGELISM (500 series)

VI YOUTH LEADERSHIP (600 series)

VII SPECIAL STUDY (700 series)

A "Certificate of Credit" is awarded for each completed course. A "Workers' Training Diploma" is awarded for the completion of five courses in one of the above classifications. A "Master Christian Service Training Diploma" is awarded for the completion of twenty courses, providing the individual has received a "Workers' Training Diploma" in Bible and one other classification.

This present course, *Dynamics of Christian Discipleship*, is the first in the Christian Living Series, No. 400.

JANUARY of each year is TRAINING MONTH in the Church of God. However, training is not, and should not, be limited to January. There should be a period of training each month in the workers' conference. Now, by popular requests for more training books, JUNE has been selected for MID-YEAR TRAINING MONTH. The Bible Series books written by Dr. Charles W. Conn will be the mid-year training courses. Plan now to complete both books—January and June of each year. The January book will meet the requirement for current certification each year; the June book does not.

A record of training should be kept in the local church of each person who studies this and other courses in the Workers'

INSTRUCTIONS FOR THE TEACHER AND STUDENT

Training Program. A record form (WTC-33) will be furnished upon request from the State Sunday School and Youth Director.

I. Instructions to the Teacher

   A. You should have completed the book and received your certificate before attempting to teach the course.

   B. The teacher will find that the book, *The Christian in the Modern World*, by T. B. Maston, will be a great assistance in preparing to teach this course. This book costs 75c and may be ordered from the Pathway Book Stores or Church of God Publishing House.

   C. Five class periods of two hours each are required to complete this book. We recommend the following lesson division of the book:

   1st lesson—Chapter 1

   2nd lesson—Chapters 2 and 3

   3rd lesson—Chapter 4, Sections I, II, and III

   4th lesson—Chapter 4, Sections IV, V, VI, and VII

   5th lesson—Chapter 4, Sections VIII, IX, and X

   The fifth lesson will take one hour. The second hour could be used for the examination or for review.

   D. A certificate will be awarded when this course is satisfactorily completed.

   E. The State Sunday School and Youth Director will furnish examination blanks. When the examination is returned to the state director, he will grade it and issue a certificate of credit.

   F. The examination should be taken with closed book.

   G. On the fifth night, a brief time should be spent in review prior to the examination.

H. It is suggested that this course of study be concluded with a special consecration service for the workers who have completed it.

II. Instructions to Students*

A. The student must attend at least four of the five class periods to be entitled to take the examination.

B. The student must read the textbook through. If the book has not been read, the instructor may permit the individual to take the examination on a pledge that the book will be read through.

C. The student should receive a grade of at least 70 on his written examination to receive credit.

As a Correspondence Course

For those who will not have the opportunity of the guidance of an instructor, or for some reason desire to study by correspondence, note the following instructions:

1. The book must be read through.

2. Have your pastor or Sunday School superintendent secure an examination for you from the state director.

3. When the examination is completed, return it to the pastor, and he will forward it to the state director.

4. The examination should be taken with closed book.

---

* Students must be fifteen years of age or older to receive credit for the course.

AUTHOR'S PREFACE

Modern man has changed the term "Christian" to meet his own desires. In many circles, the term no longer means a true believer in Jesus Christ: one who has forsaken all, denied himself, taken up the Cross, and is daily following Jesus Christ. It is the author's conviction that one must return to the original term which described the early followers of Christ to properly define the Christian experience. This book brings the terms "disciples" and "Christian" together because it is believed that an understanding of Christian discipleship will give a proper perspective to the whole of Christian living.

A declaration that Jesus Christ has all power prefaced the Great Commission, and it was climaxed by the promise that Christ would always be with His people. The strength of the early church came when they discovered that life is a cooperative venture with God. This changed the disciples into Christlike men, who became a powerful force for truth in the world. With one voice they proclaimed Christ's death and resurrection; in "one accord" they witnessed of His living presence. All division vanished, and they went forth to bear witness in the power of unity. With this clearly in mind, believers, today, must go forth living the Word in every area of life. Then it is easy to sacrifice; then it is easy to serve; then it is easy to live and to walk the way of Christian discipleship.

Many individuals have influenced the mind of the author in the preparation of this small volume: relatives, friends, authors, teachers. In an effort to acknowledge this debt, the author wishes to express gratitude for the contributions made that could not be expressed in the footnotes. A special note of appreciation is due the author's wife, Peggy, for her understanding and patience. Mrs. Rosayln M. Bosynak and J. Martin Baldree, Jr., are gratefully acknowledged for their work in the final preparation of the manuscript.

Scripture references are placed in the footnote section to conserve space; however, the reader is encouraged to read these from the King James text to receive full benefit from the author's comment.

—*Hollis L. Green*

Hialeah, Florida
October 2, 1962

CONTENTS

Foreword 7

Study Course for Sunday School and Youth Workers   8

Instructions for the Teacher and Student 9

Author's Preface 11

1. Dawn of a New Discipline 15
   (Ethical teachings of Jesus)

2. Dialogue With Deity 35
   (Man's personal relationship with God and man through Jesus Christ)

3. Dynamics of Discipleship 49
   (The affect of Jesus Christ on the lives and deeds of men)

4. Decalogue of Duty 63
   (Ten basic obligations of life)

Bibliography 111

Chapter One

DAWN OF A NEW DISCIPLINE

Since the flaming sword barred the gate to Eden, man has traveled a maze of pathways in his search for the tree of life. The human family had long awaited a "Messiah Man." The centuries of sin, after the Fall, had multiplied the evils of man, and all efforts at self-improvement had failed. Providence provided a solution to man's dilemma—Jesus Christ—the Way to God!

God had prepared a time for Jesus to be born. Israel had been prepared by prophecy and promise to be the cradle of a new faith. Judaism was a decaying religion, but it still possessed faith in one God, the highest standard of ethics and family life, and an expectation of the Messiah. Furthermore, the road system designed for marching Roman legions could be used for missionary pioneers of the new faith, and the Roman peace would, for a season, protect the first disciples of Jesus Christ. The time for Christ had come.

Look again at the times. They were full of trouble and despair for Israel and the world system. The Roman peace was kept by a ruthless military dictatorship conjoined with a corrupt religious system. The seeds of its destruction however, had already been planted by their persecuting the Jews, and it would soon turn its fury loose on converts of the new faith. The world seemed destitute of truth and buried in the gross darkness of the times.

I. DEGREES OF DARKNESS

The new discipline to be declared by Jesus Christ was not to begin in a religious vacuum. The men of the world were not found wanting for something to believe. The new faith would have to fight against entrenched religious beliefs which had existed for centuries. Most of the religious beliefs had degenerated into feeble superstitions and meaningless rituals; others seemed to be new and vigorous.

Despair of Pagan Society[1]

The religious beliefs of pagan society bred superstition and fear. The moral decadence, revealed by the writers of this period, was unbelievable. Most of the world lived in the shadow of death. The light was as darkness and the corrupting forces of evil worked beneath the surface of world order.

Animism. The primitive religion of man was animism which was based on fear. The belief seemed to be that everything that existed was a god and that the sum total of these gods was the true God. Each family had its own gods. The farmer worshiped the gods of his own farm and fireside. These individual gods personified the forces with which the individual had to deal in living his daily life. The cities of the Roman Empire had their own deities and religious festivities, but the cities soon declined and the people abandoned faith in gods that were unable to aid them against outside forces.

State and Emperor Worship. The Roman conquest had caused decline in the worship of various individual and city deities and gradually there was an increased ascription of superhuman honors to individuals. The growing power of the state and its rulers on the lives of men paved

---

[1] Merrill C. Tenney, *New Testament Survey*. (Grand Rapids: Wm. B. Eerdmans Publishing Company, 1961), pp. 65 ff.

DAWN OF A NEW DISCIPLINE

the way for a new type of religion, the worship of the state and the emperor. In this approach to religion, the ruler of the state represented "god" and his subjects were compelled to worship him. The refusal of Christians to participate in such worship later precipitated violent persecution, because Christians have always objected to worshiping a human being or any other creature.

Mystery and Magic. The state religion and emperor worship did not prove satisfying to the people, because it was a collective effort and could not be individually maintained. There was no fellowship with deity and no personal comfort or strength for the times offered to the individual. Men seemed to be seeking a more personal faith that would bring them into immediate contact with deity, and they were ready for any sort of experience that would promise them that contact.

The times gave rise to *mysticism*.[2] There were several mystic religions that became prominent.[3] They offered an outlet for emotion and satisfied the desire for personal experience and social equality. They had ritual, formulas, symbols and secret brotherhoods where all met on a common level. These mysterious religions were emphatically personal, but utterly failed to meet man's basic needs and further complicated his approach to the true God.

Similar to the mystic religions was *occultism* which enveloped forms of magic and superstitious observances that ensnared the people of pagan societies. The practitioners of such magic believed the entire world to be inhabited by spirits and demons who could be commanded to do one's bidding if only the correct magic rite or formula was used. Foretelling the future through various

---
[2] "Mysticism is a sign of the world-weariness and deep religious need that mark the decay of the old world." *Encyclopaedia Britannica* (1958 ed.), XVI, 51.

[3] The Eleusianian mysteries of Eastern origin; the Great Mother cult of Asia; Iris and Osiris from Egypt; Mithraism from Persia.

superstitions, the work of sorcerers and the mania for horoscopes reached their peak during the force of these magic religions.

Not one of man's religions had solved his problems or answered his questions about himself or his God. The search for these answers must continue.

Darkness of Man's Philosophy

The false religions of pagan society gave men no hope. Thoughtful men abandoned such religious systems altogether and began to search for a new way to explain themselves and the universe. The empty ritualism and ignorant superstition of false religions had not only complicated man's religious spirit, but caused some to deny that such a spirit existed. Thinking men began an attempt to correlate all existing knowledge about the universe into systematic form and to integrate human experience with it. Their hope was to attain full comprehension of the mysteries of which they were a part.

To achieve this end, various systems of philosophy were created.[4] Some dealt with abstract concepts of the world; others promised salvation by knowledge. New systems of thought appeared which were based on a portion of a preceding philosophy. Certain philosophies could find neither purpose nor design in a world of chance, and they advocated "pleasure" as the highest possible good. Some supplied a philosophic justification for doing what most people did anyway. Some thinkers taught that the world was controlled by an Absolute Reason and that conformity was the highest good. Self-control was the goal of others. Some abandoned all standards and convictions and became complete individualists in an effort to demonstrate that they were "different." Some dealt with ethics; others with intellect. None, however, ar-

---

[4] Platonism, Gnosticism, Neo-Platonism, Epicureanism, Stoicism, Cynicism, Skepticism.

rived at the truth that God is the ultimate standard by which man must measure himself and his actions.

Man's philosophy left him destitute of moral and spiritual purpose. The grand truth of monotheism (one God) was obscured as man groped in despair. The world by its own wisdom could not know the true God. Man could not search out His ways. And even when man's reason did glimpse the truth of one living God, he could not determine how He was to be worshiped or what relations God desired to maintain with mankind. Man at his best was far enough from truth to be in gross error. He was still without God and needed a Saviour![5]

Dim Twilight of Judaism

The Saviour was to come through Israel, but the remaining light of Judaism was a twilight of the evening and not of the morning. The Israelite nation had grown old and its vital spirituality had changed into a lifeless formalism. Israel was a weak nation and had lost all political independence to mighty Rome. Yet the embers of Messianic hope survived the never-ending succession of catastrophies. Judaism's God was different from the gods of the religions of the Roman Empire, and faith in this God was the sustaining power. Judaism was free from the worst excesses of the pagan world, but it knew but little of a pure and religious devotion, a spiritual and acceptable service. Israel was strangely backward in the philosophy and science of the day, but compared with other people, the Jews stood in "the twilight of truth." The last pages of the Old Testament terminates the words of their hope and promises: "The Lord, whom ye seek, shall suddenly come. . . ."[6] Those persons who kept this expectation were not disappointed. The New Testament

---
[5] H. D. M. Spence and Joseph S. Exell. *The Pulpit Commentary* (Grand Rapids: Wm. B. Eerdmans Publishing Company, 1950), XVI, 25.
[6] Malachi 3:1.

opens with the news of the divine daybreak—the coming of the Christ child.

II. DAWN OF SACRED DUTY

The twilight of Judaism's truth was eclipsed by the darkness of the times, but beneath the despair of the people was the slumbering force of indestructible hope. Israel looked toward the night but hoped for the bright and morning star. The birth of Jesus was the divine daybreak that was to bring the dawn of sacred duty to all men.

Divine Daybreak

The dayspring from on high was to give light to those who sat in darkness and in the shadow of death and to guide their feet in the way of peace.[7] The gaze of preceding generations had fixed their spiritual hope on the coming Messiah. No generation in the history of man had needed salvation and peace more than the one in which Jesus was born. An evening of darkness hovered about Bethlehem and the world slept in despair. It was time for the "true Light" to penetrate the night and to point the way to God. The "Sun of righteousness" promised by Malachi was to dispel the darkness, and the divine sunrise was to bring light to the earth. The good news was first given to the sleeping shepherds who were in the fields near Bethlehem, but since that glorious daybreak the news has been carried to the uttermost part of the earth.

Dawn of Duty

The angelic pronouncement of the Messiah's advent and the harmony of the heavenly hosts that told of peace

---
[7] Luke 1:78, 79 Dayspring (*anatole*) "the rising of the sun"; here "the dawn"; elsewhere in the New Testament "the east."

on earth and good will among men compelled the shepherds to investigate immediately. The shepherds were among the common folk who hated war and the personal strife caused by the sins of man and who longed for personal peace with God and true peace among their fellow men. The birth of the Messiah would change all this. Note the sequence of the actions of the shepherds: without delay they searched for and worshiped the Christ child; made known the angelic message; caused others to marvel at the wonderful news; returned to their routine tasks glorifying and praising God that they were a part of such an occasion.[8] The angelic host and the personal magnetism of Jesus had transformed the sleeping shepherds into shouting saints. They had been trusted with a heavenly message, and they had told it well. Thus, the common man had been awakened to his sacred duty—seek and worship Christ the Saviour!

For many years wise men had searched the limits of their human knowledge and had probed the unlimited reaches of the heavens for a sign to guide them in their worship of a true God. With the first glimpse of the Star of Bethlehem came the dawn of sacred duty to the wise men, and they were constrained by "His Star" to search for and to worship the newborn King.

Daylight of a Life

At the first cry of the Christ child, God had sent into the world a life that would be "the light of men." As the angelic proclamation had pointed the shepherds to the Saviour and as the star had guided the wise men to Bethlehem, the very life and redemptive activity of Jesus Christ was to bring men to God. His life was a life of quality. It was a sinless life nurtured in Nazareth, a most unlikely place for holy development. It was the custom of Jesus to attend the synagogue regularly and to be

---
8 Luke 2:8-18.

taught the discipline of Judaism.[9] He shared with other Jewish boys the thrill of the ancient Scriptures, and at the age of twelve He became a "son of the law" and visited the Temple in Jerusalem. Already His maturing sense of dedication was evident as He went about to do His heavenly Father's business with no effort to gain a personal reputation.[10] When God took upon Himself the form of human flesh, it was no longer necessary that man be utterly depraved. In the perfect life of Jesus Christ, redemption had appeared.

III. DIVINE TEACHER

The years passed in silence after His visit to the Temple until the time that He was baptized in Jordan by John to "fulfill all righteousness." Just as He had shared with the human family a body of flesh, a normal family life, and the discipline of growth, now He shares the new hope that is prevalent in Galilee and is baptized to prepare for His active ministry of teaching. He purposely allies Himself with the best of His generation and publicly identifies Himself with the new religious force that demands repentance and righteousness.

Jesus made no public claim to deity in His early ministry, but at the wedding in Cana He wrought what John describes as the "beginning of His signs" of Sonship. He then traveled to Jerusalem and cleansed the Temple of the money-changers and claimed that His future death and resurrection was His authority. He began to teach in the synagogues and to answer questions concerning the meaning and application of the commandments, the correct teachings of the resurrection, and to give judgment in legal matters.[11] This corresponds with

9 Luke 4:16.
10 Luke 2:46, 47; Philippians 2:7.
11 Luke 12:13.

the normal work of the Jewish Rabbi (teacher), who was theologian and jurist.

Divine Authority

The divine authority of Jesus Christ is the foundation of His teaching. He made pronouncements on matters commonly regarded as carrying divine sanction—the Sabbath, forgiveness, and the Temple. He frequently said, "Verily, verily, I say unto you, . . ." echoing the divine "amen" of ancient days. He proclaimed with directness and authority the nearness of the Kingdom and called for immediate decision on the part of the listeners. He repeatedly challenged the sacred Torah:[12] "Ye have heard that it hath been said by them of old time . . . but I say unto you. . . ." Although He was a Jew, He was loyal to Judaism only when Judaism was loyal to the truth. He never confused truth and tradition and placed His loyalty to the Father before His loyalty to Judaism. He did not challenge the authority of the written law, but supplemented it with additional divine utterance making it more demanding. The authority of Jesus was evidenced by His refusal to argue or to debate. He simply declared the truth of His discipline and the truth stood for itself. This is authority!

The authority of Jesus differed profoundly from that of the Jewish Rabbis. The rabbi was an interpreter of Scripture who always spoke from derived authority. The teaching of Jesus was never merely interpretation of a given sacred text. He used the Law and quoted or referred to sacred Scripture at least four hundred times in

---

[12] The Torah is the first division of the Hebrew canon and contains the five books of the Law. In addition to the written Torah, the Pharisees and rabbis recognized an oral Torah (law) which comprised specific applications of the principles of the written law. Oral traditions had become so minute and devoid of spiritual meaning as to set aside the Law of God (Matthew 15:2; Mark 7:9, 18; Colossians 2:8).

His teaching,[13] but He spoke from His own authority. There was nothing in contemporary Judaism that corresponded to the immediacy with which Jesus taught. The authority of God and the reality of His will were always directly present and fulfilled in Jesus Christ.

Jesus was different from the other teachers of His day. Every fact reveals this distinction. There was an active freshness about His teaching. He taught in the synagogues and traveled as an intenerant along the roads of Palestine, but others had taught in the open and used some of the same methods. The difference was the Man and His message. The uniqueness of Jesus is clearly seen in what He taught and in who He was. A strange crowd pressed upon Him everywhere He traveled: in open fields, by a seashore, or atop a hill the common people gathered in multitudes to hear His words of wisdom. Farmers and fishermen were taught by Him; little children felt at ease in His presence; sinners who heard Him found forgiveness and a new hope. Even the officials of Judaism who heard Him said, "Never a man spake like this man." In the course of His teaching, He healed the sick, forgave sins, fed the hungry, and calmed the elements of nature. His teaching and conduct made Him a man of distinction, a teacher different from anyone the people had seen or heard.

Demonstration of Deity

Jesus demonstrated His deity in numerous ways. In addition to His voice of divine authority, He healed the sick, worked miracles, and forgave sins. The people knew He was different, but the opinion of the people concerning Him was divided.[14] Some thought because of His miraculous power that He was John the Baptist raised from

---

[13] F. B. Meyer, *The Sermon on the Mount*. (Grand Rapids: Baker Book House, 1959), p. 49.
[14] John 7:40-43.

DAWN OF A NEW DISCIPLINE

the dead. His prophetic authority caused some to think He was Elijah. A few even thought He was Jeremiah because of His tenderness. They knew He was no ordinary prophet, but they had not grasped the truth of His deity. Jesus had not claimed to be the Messiah because the term could easily be misunderstood. Even when John had sent Jesus a perplexed inquiry from prison asking if He was the Messiah, Jesus answered with a description of the things that were taking place in His ministry. The disciples of John were instructed to tell Him: "The blind receive their sight, and the lame walk, the lepers are cleansed, and the deaf hear, the dead are raised up, and the poor have the gospel preached to them."[15] Jesus chose to demonstrate His deity and to impress upon each individual the fact that He was the Son of God. In some instances Jesus waited for the truth of His deity to break its own light upon the heart of man. On one occasion in Jerusalem a number of Jews gathered about Him in the Temple and asked: "How long dost thou make us to doubt? If thou be the Christ, tell us plainly." Jesus answered: "The works that I do in my Father's name, they bear witness of me."[16] When the light of this truth finally broke into the inner circle of His disciples, Jesus had reached the point toward which He had worked for nearly three years. It was revealed to Simon Peter that Jesus was "the Christ, the Son of the living God." With the Twelve convinced of His Sonship, He could proceed on the course that would lead Him to the cross.

IV. DISCIPLINE DECLARED

Looking at the tragic need of His world, Jesus could have thought the task of changing its course in the direction of righteousness a formidable one. Yet Jesus did not

---
15 Matthew 11:3-5.
16 John 10:24, 25.

hesitate to put Himself to God's redemptive work. The first step was to set in motion efforts to build new men for a new society. To do this Jesus declared a new and a more demanding discipline for mankind.

Discipline Defined

Discipline is defined as the "system of rules affecting conduct or action," and it "implies instruction and correction, the training which improves, molds, strengthens, and perfects character. It is the moral education obtained by the enforcement of obedience through supervision and control. . . . The purpose of discipline is the correction, the improvement, the obedience, the faith, and the faithfulness of God's child."[17]

The discipline of Jesus was addressed to the inner man—what man should be in desire and in thought. Jesus recognized the acts of men as expressions of their inner life and taught accordingly. He seemed to be more interested in persons than precepts. The truth is that the new discipline was qualitatively a new and a different attitude.[18] Jesus avoided rigid concepts that could not be universally applied, and He placed in the mind and heart the true seeds of religious thought that would grow and flower with faith, maturity, and experience. Teaching principles rather than specific rules gave the discipline of Jesus Christ validity and permanency and confined His teaching to eternal values devoid of the legalistic Judaism characteristic of His time.[19]

The eyes of Jesus penetrated the very life of man and saw him exactly as he was. With no reservation, Jesus

---

[17] Everett F. Harrison, Geoffrey W. Bromile, and Carl F. H. Henry, *Baker's Dictionary of Theology*. (Grand Rapids: Baker Book House, 1960), p. 167. Used by permission.

[18] Gunther Bornkamm, *Jesus of Nazareth*. (New York: Harper and Brothers, translation of the third edition, 1959), p. 108.

[19] Henlee H. Barnette, *Introducing Christian Ethics*. (Nashville: Broadman Press, 1961), p. 42.

described man frankly and sincerely. Note the procession of unlovely people that parade through His teaching, each clearly exposed because of divine discernment: a rude neighbor refuses bread, an unwise farmer has no thought of the future, a high-living glutton ignores the beggar, an impatient youth deserts home; a judge rules unjustly, a steward juggles his books, a lazy servant buries his talent, a heartless banker forecloses on a widow's mortgage, and an envious farmer sows tares in a neighbor's crop.[20]

There was a positiveness in the discipline of Jesus that was lacking in other religious teachings. Two basic characteristics contributed to the inspirational power and effectiveness of His discipline: (1) The discipline of Jesus had a religious basis, deriving its imperative from the divine nature and will. It had a divine goal—to make trust in God the root and principle of all goodness and to make men in the image of Christ. (2) The discipline of Jesus was exemplified in His own life. He taught as effectively by example as He did by precept. Discipleship or following Christ came to mean not only the acceptance of certain principles of right and compliance with their demands, but a supreme loyalty to a Person in whom these principles had received concrete embodiment and fulfillment. There is no parallel to the personal influence of Jesus Christ in the affairs of men.[21]

Jesus defined the essential quality of a moral act by teaching the principle of love and the law of right conduct.[22] The concept of right conduct presupposes the law of love and is distinctive from it. The law of love produces right conduct. It is the motive alone which gives moral quality to action. This absolute inwardness of mor-

---

[20] Reginald E. O. White, *The Stranger of Galilee*. (Grand Rapids: Wm. B. Eerdmans Publishing Company, 1960), p. 78.

[21] Albert C. Knudson, *The Principles of Christian Ethics*. (New York: Abingdon-Cokesbury Press, 1943), p. 37.

[22] Luke 10:27; Mark 12:28-31.

al law is the underlying theme of the teachings of Jesus. With Jesus, the heart was the seat of all virtue and the spring of all truly righteous conduct.[23]

The unique way Jesus proclaimed this view had momentous consequences both negative and positive. (1) He broke with judaism and His own people by rejecting their ceremonialism and legalism and by declaring a positive and an active religious force which is divinely imparted to the heart of man. (2) These factors led to a profound emphasis on moral purity and on a lofty moral ideal. It was this fact that transformed love into holy love and gave the Christian doctrine of love its comprehensiveness.[24]

Development of the Discipline

The quality of simplicity distinguished the discipline of Jesus. The basic appeal of His teaching is always in an innate knowledge of the truth, to the inner discernment, the moral sense of ordinary folk. He talked of the heavenly Father who loves and reigns. He discoursed of life within the Father's family, of brotherliness, sympathy, forgiveness, and love. He opened up endless possibilities of the power of prayer and the victories of faith. "Whatever problems His words may raise, of faith or more often of obedience, we rarely are in doubt of what He means. Our difficulties . . . are not in understanding but in doing."[25]

The methods used to advance the development of His discipline often caused His listeners to admit the truth being taught or provoked the recognition of truth by the listener's own thought processes. Jesus was effective in His use of short pointed statements to stimulate basic understanding of His discipline. He posed innumerable

---

23 Knudson, *loc. cit.*
24 *Ibid.*
25 White, *op. cit.*, p. 76.

DAWN OF A NEW DISCIPLINE

questions to relate outward conduct to inward character. In the course of His teaching He used conversions to teach that He Himself was the forgiver.

Jesus had a dramatic force in His manner of telling a story to illustrate the truth He taught, and He used an exceptional economy of words. The parables which Jesus told contained hidden truths. He used this simple method to explain eternal truths and was usually easily understood by the average listener, because He took His stories from everyday circumstances.

No rapid summary we may give can do justice to the wealth of meaning contained in the parables of Jesus, but if we see them as a whole, their method will be illumined and their message crystallized. Understand the parables and you will understand the basic message of Jesus to mankind. R. E. O. White gives this summary:

> Not the whole circle of Christian truth can be found within their frame, but all that is essential to practical discipleship is illustrated here: the nature of the Kingdom and its coming to the heart; its laws of service, diligence, and love, the meaning and necessity of grace, God's answer to man's sin; the need of prayer; and certainity of final judgment on the misused life. And through them all there breathes the unmistakable assurance that in Himself and in His Word men, if they choose, can find salvation.[26]

The essential elements of character expected by Jesus are expressed in the Beatitudes.[27] Those who were brought under the new discipline must be bankrupt in spirit and utterly dependent on God, penitent of sin and willing to share the burdens of others, Christ-controlled

---
26 White, *op. cit.*, p. 85. Used by permission.
27 Matthew 5:3-11.

and ready to obey, earnestly desirous of the righteousness of God; merciful, truly righteous with no mixed motives, a peacemaker and able to joy in suffering and persevere during persecution.

The character produced by the new discipline was to result in spiritual influence. This is the divine intention of Jesus. Those who live in the attitude of the Beatitudes will realize a threefold law of influence: (1) Salt—that preserves and prevents corruption. (2) Light—that points the way. (3) City—the realization of social order and progress. Then He adds that these disciples will be a light shining before men because of their good works and will influence others to glorify the heavenly Father.[28]

Demands of the Discipline

The strongly worded principles of Jesus in His Sermon on the Mount have served as a practical guide to turn men's minds more strongly to His teaching and have incorporated the spirit of them into men's daily lives. Two characteristics of the righteousness required are prominent:

(1) *Jesus demanded an exceeding righteousness.* A firm requirement of the new discipline is a new righteousness that exceeds that of the scribes and Pharisees.[29] Jesus declared that the Kingdom's righteousness was superior to that practiced by the moralists in the Jewish community.[30] He affirms that negative goodness alone is not sufficient to meet the standard of the new discipline. External conformity to the letter of the Law was not enough. Those who would follow Jesus must have their hearts changed, for their inner selves must be consecrated to the cause of truth.

---
28 Matthew 5:13-16.
29 Matthew 5:20.
30 The most learned (scribes) and the most zealous (Pharisees) in the Law.

(2) *Jesus demanded a righteousness springing out of love.* The new discipline given and lived by Jesus Christ goes beyond Jewish law, but it does not annul it. The demands of the Law and the Prophets are not cancelled; they become flesh and blood and live among men in the person and work of Jesus Christ. Jesus exemplified the Law in His own life and gave it a higher and richer fulfillment. He took the six hundred and thirteen laws and transformed them into the "Law of Love" that was extended to include the enemy.[31] The moral dynamics of this love will yet transform the lives of men.

The importance Jesus attached to the demands of His discipline is marked by the abundance of detail with which He illustrated them. The manifesto of the Messiah on moral conduct was clear and compelling. The changes in the discipline of Jesus can be seen in His concentration on essential points of human life and in His re-evaluation of ancient values. In His Sermon on the Mount, He translated the requirements of the Law into the demands of His new discipline.[32]

(a) *Demanded more respect for the individual.* The first contrast between the Law and the new discipline was in the requirement dealing with murder. Jesus required dignity for the individual. He condemned murder, but He equally condemned anger against one's brother. Jesus stated that contempt or despising of another deserved the punishment of the highest court and that any personal insult deserved hell-fire.

(b) *Demanded more honor for womanhood.* His words on adultery are perhaps the most searching words ever uttered concerning immorality. Jesus declared that even an evil eye offends the heart and makes it guilty of im-

---

[31] Barnette, *op. cit.*, p. 45.
[32] Matthew chapters 5-7. The demands of the new discipline are based on the following verses: (1) 5:21-26; (2) 5:27-32; (3) 5:33-37; (4) 5:38-48; (5) 6:1-18; (6) 6:9-34; (7) 7:1-12.

purity. The Law permitted the breaking of the family relationship by divorce, but Jesus very pointedly stated that nothing should soil or in any way pollute marriage, the very foundation of the family and of the home.

(c) *Demanded more esteem for one's reputation.* The old standard permitted an individual to substantiate the truth with the goodness of another by swearing an oath. The new discipline declared that the character of citizens of the Kingdom should be unquestionable, making the oath unnecessary. A simple "yes" and "no" answer would be sufficient for a man who had an honest report.

(d) *Demanded more initiative in friendship.* Under the Law the neighbor was to be loved, but the enemy could be hated. Jesus gave love a new basis and an added dimension and said that revenge is to be left to God and that His followers were to love and to pray for their enemies. He required the offended to take the initiative.

(e) *Demanded true motives in worship.* The new discipline required the giving of alms as a silent part of worship to God and not openly for show. The followers of Jesus were to pray with simple faith in secret and were to expect God to bless openly their efforts. They were to live a positive life and to keep a cheerful countenance even when afflicted with the burden of fasting.

(f) *Demanded faith in the future.* The followers of Christ were not to be fearful of the future. He taught that it was unnecessary to lay up earthly treasures that would perish but that one should lay up spiritual treasures in heaven. Material gains were to be used for the advancement of the Kingdom to insure their continued desire to enter into the Kingdom. They were to have one Master and trust Him absolutely for their daily needs: food, shelter, raiment, health, employment. They were to seek the Kingdom first and to trust God with the future.

(g) *Demanded honest dealings with others.* Jesus taught that men should be concerned about others, but He warned about passing judgment on them. No individual could have all the facts; therefore, God was the Judge of all. The time should be more wisely spent examining one's own faith. The spiritual needs of others were to be considered, and a spiritual witness was to be given to those willing to listen. Jesus declared that the good things of the Father belonged to His followers, for the asking. He demanded that others be treated as they desired to be treated themselves.

The multitude on the mountain that heard Jesus make the demands of His discipline were told that the test of their character would be in the way they walked: the narrow way or the broad way. They were warned against false teachers and false fruit and told that every believer must bear fruit, and that they would be known by their fruit. Jesus declared that all profession must be practiced to substantiate it, and that the final test would be the foundation of their spiritual house: sand or rock. If the foundation was the spiritual Rock, the house would stand the storms of life. When Jesus had ended His declaration of the new discipline, the people were astonished at His doctrine: "For he taught them as one having authority, and not as the scribes."[33]

DISCUSSION GUIDE

1. What was the condition of the world at the birth of Jesus?
2. What similarity did the ministry of Jesus have with the normal work of the Jewish Rabbi? How was it different?
3. Discuss the divine authority of Jesus.
4. How did Jesus demonstrate His deity?

---

[33] Matthew 7:13-29.

5. What effect did the teaching of principles rather than specific rules have on the ethical teachings of Jesus?
6. What basic characteristics contributed to the power and effectiveness of the new discipline?
7. Discuss the demands of the new discipline.

Chapter Two

DIALOGUE WITH DEITY

Life is essentially dialogue[1] or participation—no man can live or die to himself. It was not good for man to be alone in Eden, because he was not complete in himself. Man must relate his life to others in order that he might fulfill his destiny. The most beautiful part of life in Eden is found in Adam's walking in harmony and in complete fellowship with the Creator.

Why did God make man? Man was created to keep and to dress the Garden of Eden and to satisfy the yearning of the Father heart of God. From the first inspired record of God walking with Adam in the cool of the Garden to the final vision of the New Jerusalem descending from heaven that God might dwell with men, the underlying message of the Scriptures has been of a God who desires to come forth and to meet with man.[2]

1. DIALOGUE—GOD WITH MAN

The first question of the Westminster Catechism reads: "What is the chief end of man?" The answer: "Man's chief end is to glorify God and to enjoy Him forever."

---

[1] Dialogue in this chapter means conversation between two or more persons.
[2] White, *op. cit.*, p. 16.

The story is told of a little girl that illustrates the true meaning of this answer. It seems that a godly mother, putting her child to bed, had asked the first question in the catechism and had received the proper answer. Then the mother, not quite realizing why, asked: "And darling, what do you think is the chief end of God?" Pondering a moment, the child replied: "If the chief end of man is to glorify God and enjoy Him forever, then I suppose the chief end of God must be to glorify man and to enjoy him forever." Out of the mouths of babes comes words of wisdom. The Word of God confirms this to be true. God's delight is with His creation. It is clear that fellowship with a redeemed man is dear to the heart of God.[3]

Conversation Through Adam

When God made man in His image, He made an intelligent being with whom He could converse about the beauties of creation. Adam was the keeper of God's garden and God talked with Him. Man today can hardly imagine the joy and refreshment of such conversation. Man was not made only to glorify God, but to enjoy God and to be God's joy. Many see only the first part and think that they must wait until after death to begin enjoying God. The conversation between God and Adam assures us that man was made to do both now. Man fulfilled his highest destiny when he communed "naked" before his Creator in the Garden. The heartbreak of God occurred when sin spoiled this holy fellowship.

Covenant Through Abraham

After the Fall, God begins to separate from the sons of men those who would listen to His voice. He longed for fellowship with the men He had made. Enoch and Noah

---
[3] Geoffrey R. King, *Truth For Our Time*. (Grand Rapids: Wm. B. Eerdmans Publishing Company, 1957), pp. 40, 41.

were said to have "walked with God," but God was searching for a man that would yield himself completely to divine will. In Abraham, God found a man to father a family and build a nation. The people of God received a covenant through Abraham—a covenant for ultimate redemption and complete restoration to fellowship with God. The divine plan to bring all men back to full fellowship was constantly marred by evil, but God set apart the descendants of Abraham as His "peculiar treasure." God's plan was to purify for Himself a people—to be peculiarly His own.[4] Through this covenant remanent God produced Jesus Christ.

Communion Through Christ

In the Gospels, God comes still nearer to man through the Incarnation.[5] The fellowship with man is placed on a more intimate basis. God sent His Son to dwell among men, and in human flesh He partook of human suffering and temptation. The participation of Jesus Christ in the affairs of man and His willingness to share the plight of the human family clearly bear witness of God's desire for communion and fellowship with man. Calvary gives this fellowship a new dimension.

At Pentecost again the Divine invades the human. The Book of Acts transports man to the present dispensation and finds God nearest of all to the human family, in the Person of the Holy Spirit, taking up His abode in blood-redeemed hearts. Until the ultimate glorification of the body, the indwelling of the Holy Ghost is the satisfying of the Father's heart for fellowship with man.

---

[4] Peculiar comes from *peculium* meaning exclusive or private property. This word is used to show the intimate relationship between God and His people. Exodus 19:5; Deuteronomy 14:2; Titus 2:4; 1 Peter 2:9.
[5] John 1:14.

II. DIALOGUE—MAN WITH GOD

It is through Jesus Christ that men can be restored to proper relationship with God the Father and can live together in Christian community. Man was made in the image of God. To dwell together in proper interpersonal relationship, he must be reconciled to God and be conformed to the image of Christ. Man must be redeemed and restored to fellowship with God before he can maintain proper relationship with other men. This is the beauty of the Christian faith—men in harmony and agreement, because they are in proper relationship with God.

Conversation Restored

The conversation between God and man was ended abruptly when man sinned. Any dialogue after this was a painful thing, and man avoided the searching experience.[6] God desired to restore man to proper fellowship with Him and to re-establish their mutually enjoyable conversation. The work on the cross brought about a conversion experience which would change the life of man and would reconcile him to God.

Calvary Encounter. God seeks to secure a personal encounter with man—a Calvary encounter. This is entering into a two-way covenant with God of absolute love and devotion, based upon redeeming love revealed in Christ. Sin separated man from God, but Calvary is the place of reconciliation.

Conversion Experience. God will step into the life of any man who will walk the Calvary road, and he will experience conversion. This experience takes place when man is made aware of his own sinful, self-centered nature and confronts the Incarnate God at Calvary. Man's

---

[6] Paul M. Miller, *Group Dynamics in Evangelism.* (Scottdale, Pennsylvania: Herald Press, 1958), p. 135.

will is bowed and redirected toward God in total surrender and fusion with the will of God, and his emotions are stirred by this tremendous experience. The Calvary encounter or conversion is completed when man, seeking to find realization and fulfillment of his essential nature, accepts forgiveness of sins and is restored to fellowship with God.[7]

When anyone takes the step by faith toward God he is transformed, and he can again enjoy the original conversation with God. Man must put himself on record as being committed to the will of God which cannot merely be an outward compliance or external submission, but must be a completely and sincerely forsaking of sins and a devoted following of Jesus. However, though the will of God is the turning point in submission, the Son of God is the turning Person.[8] Jesus Christ is the Mediator between God and man.

Companionship With Christ

A genuinely Christian person is living each moment in personal fellowship with God through Jesus Christ.[9] Converted and identified with Christ, the believer begins to enjoy true companionship with Deity. He becomes a partaker or sharer of the divine nature and a joint heir with Jesus. The personal encounter of the believer continues to be a searching experience in the life of every Christian. Jesus Christ becomes the believer's living contemporary to share constantly life's daily problems.

God calls men to absolute conformity to the image of Christ. Nothing less than this did God propose and with nothing less should the believer be content.[10] God called

---
[7] Miller, *op. cit.*, p. 138.
[8] Robert A. Cook, *Steps to Maturity*. (Wheaton: Scripture Press Foundation, 1960), pp. 6, 7.
[9] Miller, *loc. cit.*
[10] Herbert F. Stevenson (ed.), *Keswick's Authentic Voice*. (Grand Rapids: Zondervan Publishing House, 1959), p. 254.

man to fellowship with His Son on earth, both in His sufferings and His joys. The object of God's call is that man might be holy now and have full fellowship with Him. As man draws nearer to God the Father, he is conscious of the divine presence and companionship with the risen Lord. His countenance radiates the glow of God's glory. The believer's faith gives substance to the presence of Christ until the very words of his prayers, by faith, are as satisfying as if the Master's garment had been touched.

III. DIALOGUE—MAN WITH MAN

A man who has never been redeemed and restored to fellowship with God has been deprived of his full personality development and is constantly in difficulty with others. However, when men are converted they come to know each other as new creatures in Christ, and they have taken the first step toward developing satisfying human relations. When Christ becomes the center of men's lives and divine love becomes the force of lives no disturbance can alter their living relationship.

Circle of Human Experience[11]

From the Christian point of view, the center of all things is divine love. With this in mind, let us look at the full circle of human experience and relationship.

The First Half-Circle. The starting point of the first half-circle of man's experience is the individual. Man either thinks of himself or of others, and his attitude is determined by his relationship with God. In this part of the circle of human relationships, man usually uses others to his own advantage. There is little or no regard for the privileges and rights of others when they distract from

---
[11] J. H. Oldham, *Life Is Commitment*. (New York: Association Press, 1959 Abridgment), p. 28 ff.

personal desires. The "we" of joint activity may only be the enlargement of the "I" and not really mean anything. A corporate task may be credited to the leader with no mention of those who actually made the accomplishment. In this half-circle, everything seems to focus on the individual.

The Second Half-Circle. In the second half-circle of human experience man relates himself to others. The essence of man is not in man himself. This can be found only when he is associated with others in the unity of man with man. Proper relationship with other persons is basic to the whole circle of human experience and activity. Man is essentially man with man and life is continued involvement with others in mutually related tasks. When man is restored to fellowship with God, he cannot live in complete loneliness and solitude. His experience can not long remain a solitary thing. He must become concerned with others. The Christian must build a satisfying relationship with all men.

Christian Concept of Man

This brings us to the ultimate question: What is the Christian concept of man? One school of thought tries to understand man as he relates to the rest of the world. When this idea is accepted, man loses all value and meaning and becomes just another part of the world of "things." The proper attitude is illustrated by those who would interpret the world in terms of man. They believe that God made the beauties of earth and then placed man there to enjoy both the Creator and the creation.[12] This question cannot be completely answered without considering the one perfect Man, Jesus Christ. For the Christian, the point of decision is the revelation of the manifestation of the true and perfect man in Jesus Christ.

---
12 Oldham, *op. cit.*, p. 44.

Man is the creation of God, corrupted by sin and separated from divine fellowship; however, through Jesus Christ, man can be reconciled to God and can be restored to full fellowship.

A Christian concept of man must rest on one's concept of Christ. He was unmistakably, the Man *with* men, the Man for men. This fact for the Christian must be decisive.[13] The Christian must accept no ethical teaching that is recognized to be contrary to the revealed Word and the will of God. The written Word is always the criterion by which the thoughts and deeds of men are evaluated. The only perfect standard for man is revealed in Jesus Christ. To attain this ideal, every man must accept the atoning death, the bodily resurrection and the continuing advocacy of Jesus. In addition to the regenerating and sanctifying powers of truth, man needs the enlightening power of the Word of God and the enabling work of the Holy Spirit to become "a perfect man, unto the measure of the stature of the fulness of Christ."[14]

Christian Contact With Man

The will of God brings men into contact with others. The believer must be certain that this contact measures up to Christian standards. Living in harmony with others, assisting them, being a Christian example, and cooperating with them for the common good is the Christian minimum.[15] A joint encounter of believers, like radii of a circle forms a togetherness with Christ as its center. Here men can dwell in love, worship God, and participate in Christian activity. This happens because men are willing to commit themselves to Christ and to take their stand together for Christian conduct.[16]

---

[13] Oldham, *op. cit.*, p. 45.

[14] C. B. Eavey, *Principles of Christian Ethics*. (Grand Rapids: Zondervan Publishing House, 1958), p. 111.

[15] Cook, *op. cit.*, p. 10.

[16] Miller, *op. cit.*, p. 146.

Figure 1   **Figure 2**   **Figure 3**

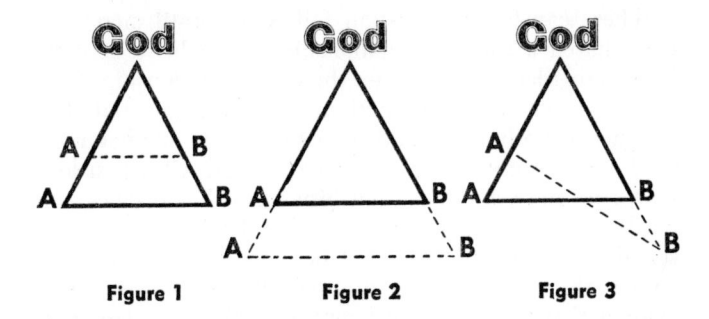

TRIANGLE RELATIONSHIP. The relationship between A and B illustrated here is in direct relation to their relationship with God. Figure 1 shows that as A and B get closer to God they are closer to one another. Figure 2 illustrates the strain in human relations when both A and B drift away from God. Figure 3 shows the change that takes place when A draws closer to God and B drifts away. This situation often complicates both the spiritual life and the human relations of A and B.

Christian Triangle Encounter. The triangular relationship among Christians is insisted upon in the Scriptures. The man who loves God must love his brother. The closer men get to God the more intimate and more harmonious their relationship becomes with each other. The converse is true: when men drift from God there is a deterioration in their human relations (see figures 1, 2, and 3). The language of the prayer Jesus taught His followers gives evidence of His collective concern for the disciples. He taught them to pray: "Our Father . . . Give us . . . forgive us . . . as we forgive . . . lead us . . . deliver us. . . ." When men are in full fellowship with God, they have a burning desire to live peaceably with all men. The problem of the unredeemed is that no amount of "human engineering" can simulate the spiritual fellowship of believers.

There can be no Christian fellowship until men have first shared a common relationship with Christ. It must be a triangular encounter—a three-way relationship. Men may associate with one another in daily living, but they will never really know and understand one another until they meet together in the presence of God. Christian love leaves no room for the usual bitterness that plagues and weakens human relations. A life of love causes one to see the connection between God and man and demonstrates the real meaning of one's life in Christ. It is evident that the more one knows of Christ and His love, the more love he will have both for Christ and for his fellow men.

Fellowship with God is the key to proper human relations. This is the subject of the First Epistle of John. John declares that the basis of spiritual fellowship is fellowship with the Father through a union with Jesus Christ. Believers who live and walk in the true Light of God will have fellowship with God, and once this fellowship is established we can be assured of a satisfying relationship with others. Without fellowship with God, our lives cannot be essentially right.

Harmony in human relations often depends on what one is making of his own life. The structure of life must be built upon the Word of God; however, inter-personal relations depend on (1) the climate of one's personality, (2) the standards by which others are measured, and (3) the basic motives that determine one's acts. The Christian experience meets the needs in each of these areas. When people join together in an effort to build their lives after God's plan, they are bound to get along with each other.[17]

A wrong relationship with God is the root of all unchristian conduct. God desires that men live together in the "realm of redemption." Sin in the life of an in-

---

[17] Cook, *op. cit.*, pp. 11, 14.

dividual causes his relationship with God to be changed, and his relationship with others disturbed. Likewise any disturbance in the personal relations of two believers hinders their spiritual fellowship with God.[18] It is a three-way interaction, a triangular relationship or nothing.

Men often think that they are having trouble with their fellow men, when actually they themselves are out of touch with God and are in trouble spiritually. These differences often lead to the "futile fuss of talk." It should be remembered that a sinner is the victim of his own nature and quarrels because he cannot help himself. It takes the work of divine authority to correct this, but it can be done through simple faith in God. God can change the diverse fractions of human behavior into the common denominator of His grace through Jesus Christ. Transformed by the power of His cross, the will of God becomes clearly seen, human barriers melt away, and men with varying personalities can bow together in worship and in love. It is in Jesus Christ that men get together; He is the *one access route for all men* to the Father. When men sincerely pray about differences, they will discover that the positive virtues flowing out of their Christian love causes them to join forces to do God's will.

When men are transformed by God's redemptive love and are gathered into Christian community, they are eager to co-operate for edification and for evangelism. As the Spirit of God weaves the scarlet thread of redemptive benefits into the pattern of their interpersonal relations, Christians grow in spiritual companionship and in concern for others.

Companionship With Christians. A dynamic, growing, transforming Christian experience compels men into Christian companionship. Redeemed men work together in group life and activity, but they always remain an individual on a personal basis with God. Walking with

[18] 1 Peter 3:7.

other believers in Christian fellowship is a searching experience. The believer accepts his new companions as new creatures in Christ, and his forgiven sins are forgotten. While there remains a clear distinction between persons, yet men set apart from the world assume a common identity and bond of peace in the Spirit. Fellowship that is Christian sanctifies all of life and creates a oneness among believers.[19] This God-created unity is not meant to make believers into unhappy "satellite souls" burdened by the monotony of similarity, but it is concerned with the believers' common devotion to Christ, their mutual fellowship, and their united action for Christ.[20]

The spiritual life of man could not long remain a solitary thing. The believer must not only have a relationship with God, but he must have fellowship with other Christians. The Christian experience becomes void if it is deprived of fellowship with other believers. Should Christians discover one another in an unchurched community, they should not think of the church as being "back home," but they should unite to function as a vital part of the living church. Saints experience great joy when they unite and then watch the emerging church growing out of their having gathered together in Christ.

Christians dwelling together in fellowship form a spiritual community that demonstrates the love of Christ. Since love must first be learned by experiencing love, God teaches man to love by first loving Him. "He that loveth is born of God and knoweth God." The Christian finds his basic need for inter-personal love and companionship met by the divine love and Christian fellowship. Because of God's indwelling love, Christians love one another with a fervency and a purity unattainable by any other group on earth.

---

[19] Miller, *op. cit.*, p. 144.
[20] Cook, *op. cit.*, p. 14.

There is a creativeness in Christian companionship. God ministers His own strength to a believer by sending him assistance through a fellow Christian. The primary concern of God's plan for perfecting the saints is to make them in the image of Christ. When Christians assist one another in spiritual growth, they share with God this effort to make men like Himself.[21]

Christians have a right to expect consensus in their joint activity. Sincere Christians will be agreeable and respectable to one another even when they disagree. In search for the solution to any common problem, believers must seek the guidance of the Spirit and ask that God's will be done. They should move through a problem-solving experience with assurance that God is pointing the way. When the solution is found, they should say: "This seemed good to the Holy Ghost and to us." Observing how Christians meet the problems of life should be an evangelizing, convicting experience to sinners.[22]

Contact With the Unconverted. Believers united for common action must have Christ's redeeming concern and must relay His love to the unconverted. Evangelism is no optional service for a genuine Christian. He speaks of spiritual things with joy and with an easy naturalness. There is no pious display or morbid fear; the believer's very personality diffuses the fragrance of Christ's love and saving grace.

All men search for a person or cause worthy of their energies and loyalities. The Christian cause offers the only adequate Person or cause for complete commitment. Each believer is to be an ambassador for Christ and represent His saving grace among men. Christians are sent as Christ was sent—to plead with men. The true believer

---
21 Miller, *op. cit.*, p. 151.
22 Miller, *op. cit.*, p. 108.

will have a sense of evangelistic mission in all he does. He will feel constrained to perform his sacred duty.[23]

DISCUSSION GUIDE

1. What is the chief end of man?

2. How is a man restored to fellowship with God? How does this effect his relationship with others?

3. Why is the second half circle of human experience important to the Christian?

4. What is the Christian concept of man?

5. Discuss the triangle relationship.

---

[23] Miller, *op. cit.*, pp. 162, 166.

Chapter Three

DYNAMICS OF DISCIPLESHIP

A fundamental fact in human conduct is that every action must be motivated by some factor. This is true not only in the physical realm, but it is true even more so in man's spiritual life. A spiritual nature is man's chief possession, and when this nature is stimulated to constructive conduct man is motivated by a master passion. Jesus Christ is the motivation behind Christian discipleship. He is the dynamic force that becomes the disciple's Master power.[1]

The general picture evoked by the Gospels is one of a strong movement stirred up by Jesus among the people. Crowds pressed around Him, listened eagerly to His words, and were amazed at the authority of His teachings. They sought His healing power and praised the miracles He performed. As a result of His ministry, many persons attached themselves to Jesus in varying degrees of conviction and loyalty. This frames the many individual scenes from the story of Jesus, but these followers do not constitute His disciples. To follow someone from place to place does not mean discipleship.

I. DISCIPLESHIP DEFINED

A disciple is a pupil or a learner who comes under

---

[1] J. Clyde Yates, *Our Marching Orders in Evangelism*. (New York: The American Press, 1957), pp. 56, 57.

the discipline of another. The disciple learns certain principles from his teacher and maintains them on the teacher's authority. The term involves a combination of ideas of learning and of serving and even leaves room for elements of immaturity and imperfection. It is a term appropriately related to God's original idea of creating man in His image and in His likeness. Man was created in God's image in the sense that he could share God's interests, commune with Him, and share His work in the world. Man was not like God, infinite in knowledge and in understanding, or in any of the divine attributes. Rather, man was endowed with the capacity to learn from God and to be instructed or disciplined by divine authority.

A broad and a narrow use of the term is discernible in the Gospels and is seen to the best advantage in connection with the choice of the twelve disciples.[2] This group of disciples *par excellence* was chosen from a larger company of disciples. By virtue of this selection the term disciple was narrowed to this group by traditional usage. During the ministry of Jesus, numerous others were designated as disciples.[3] Those who followed Him were commonly known as "His disciples," thus the contemporaneous description of the term has been preserved. Jesus had twelve disciples, seventy disciples, and a great multitude of disciples. There were active disciples and passive disciples, true disciples and false disciples.

Discipleship means a decision to follow Jesus Christ. It consists, in actual fact, of a determination to abandon everything so that one can follow Jesus anywhere and can accept the life and privation of a wanderer.[4] It calls for the spirit of loving devotion and requires the giving

---

[2] Luke 6:12, 13.

[3] We read of Moses' disciples (John 9:28); John's disciples (Mark 2:18); disciples of the Pharisees (Matthew 22:16).

[4] Bornkamm, *op. cit.*, p. 146.

DYNAMICS OF DISCIPLESHIP   51

of priority to the cause of Christ. In summary, a disciple is: (1) one who believes and trusts in Christ, (2) one who learns in the school of Christ, (3) one who is committed to a sacrificial life for His sake,[5] and (4) one who acts to fulfill the climactic obligation of discipleship, namely, that of making disciples of others.[6]

New Testament discipleship was not a terminal course in teacher training. It was not a transitional stage which ended with the disciple's becoming a teacher in his own right. "The disciple is not above his master, nor the servant above his lord. It is enough for the disciple that he be as his master, and the servant as his lord." These are the words of Jesus. "As his master" does not mean the promotion of the disciple to the rank of his teacher, but it refers to his readiness to bear the same abuse which the teacher encountered and to accept it as a mark of supreme distinction.[7] The Disciples were to have only one Master, and together all the followers of Christ were to learn from Him. This meaning of discipleship is clearly stated in the words of Jesus to some believing Jews: "If ye continue in my word, then are ye my disciples indeed." Jesus gave His Name to the Disciples as their authority.

The Gospels do not teach that salvation and discipleship are two distinct things, but that they are two parts of a single experience which involves one's relationship to Jesus Christ as Saviour and Lord. It is clear that Jesus taught that when one is saved he becomes a disciple. The New Testament presents Jesus as both Saviour and Lord and requires that He be accepted and followed.

The special relationship between Jesus and His disciples is in keeping with the special character of His

---
[5] Luke 14:27, 33.
[6] Matthew 28:19: the understanding seems to be "Go and make disciples."
[7] Matthew 10:24, 25; Bornkamm, *op. cit.*, pp. 144, 145.

teachings. The Disciples must be distinguished from His followers, because they were a more intimate group. It is true that what He demands from them does not in fact differ from what He asks of everybody: to repent in the light of the coming Kingdom; to abandon everything and to follow the call; to sell all for one precious pearl. This had been the call advanced to all. The difference between the Disciples and the followers can be seen in their response to the call and in the varying degrees of conviction and of loyalty.

II. DISCIPLESHIP DEMONSTRATED

Jesus was extremely popular as long as He was healing the sick and feeding the multitudes, but when the people discovered the demands of His discipline they wanted nothing more to do with Him. It seemed that Jesus was always whittling down the multitudes that followed Him. Those who were there for the "loaves and fishes" soon departed. The demands of discipleship were too difficult for them. On one occasion, Jesus even asked the disciples who remained, "Will ye also go away?" Realizing that salvation and discipleship were bound together, they answered: "To whom shall we go? Thou hast the words of eternal life." Those who remained were willing to abide by the requirements of discipleship and could be counted on to obey the commandments of Jesus.

Discipleship means decision, but it does not mean decision to follow the crowd. Originally the term "disciple" had a much broader meaning than it has now, but it did not then include everybody who listened to Jesus teach or those who were moved enough by Him to follow along with the crowd. Discipleship is a decision to believe and to follow Jesus Christ. It means complete decision to go all the way—commitment to complete the journey regardless of the cost.

Call to Discipleship. The call to discipleship goes forth to everyone and the response of each person is an act of obedience. Jesus is the Christ and has authority to call and to demand obedience to His Word. The seriousness of the call is demonstrated by the earliest disciples. Their encounter with Jesus was a testimony to His absolute and direct authority. Jesus called them and expected them to obey which resulted in salvation and discipleship. "Follow me" simply meant that they were to forsake all and to follow in the footsteps of Jesus, not that there was glory in following but that the individual may serve as a disciple. The old things forsaken with their relative security for that which seems to be absolute insecurity. However, complete abandonment to Christ becomes security and safety as one walks in the fellowship with Jesus.

Conditions of Discipleship. Men who would follow Jesus must take certain definite steps. Discipleship is a summons to one to assume an exclusive attachment to Jesus Christ. This requires proximity and priority. The first step, which follows the call, severs the individual from his previous existence and places him in a situation where faith is possible. To take the next step, the individual must "enroll" in the school of Christ and learn to live a principled life, patterned after Christ Himself.

Jesus wanted men close to Him so that He could teach them by word and by deed. Only in this way would they become His disciples. There must be a strong attachment to Jesus and to His teachings. Talking very intimately about the meaning and purpose of discipleship, Jesus stated that it was a matter of abiding in Him, and this abiding would be marked by receiving His word, by obeying His commands, and by loving one another. By this abiding, they would bear much fruit and would be His disciples indeed. Jesus declared that this kind of discipleship would glorify the Father in the world.[8]

According to the New Testament, no man can know Jesus Christ as Saviour who is not willing to know Him as Lord. "If thou shalt confess with thy mouth the Lord Jesus, and shalt believe in thine heart that God hath raised Him from the dead, thou shalt be saved." What is involved in believing that God raised Jesus from the dead? He was "declared to be the Son of God with power . . . by the resurrection from the dead." It is simply a belief in the Sonship of Jesus Christ. The confession of Christ as Lord is involved in salvation and in discipleship. When Christ becomes Lord of one's life, He rules that life. The individual gladly bows and obeys; that is discipleship. When Jesus spoke to the multitude and placed before them the demands of discipleship, He did not hesitate to ask them to forsake all and to follow Him. He was to be their Saviour and their Lord. He pointed to the cross as a mark of their discipleship and as evidence of their faith in Him.

The conditions involved in discipleship are well illustrated in these words of R. E. O. White concerning the rich young ruler:

> The rich young ruler possessed everything that compels attention—youth, wealth, excellent character, social prominence. Moreover, he was desperately in earnest. Such men do not run to kneel in public before a preaching carpenter without some urgent purpose . . . He asked for life eternal . . . a serious request, and seriously answered. Yet the young man went away deeply *grieved*.
>
> For the first time he saw himself by other standards than his own, and all his confidence and pride were suddenly destroyed. His la-

---
[8] John 15:1-17.

DYNAMICS OF DISCIPLESHIP

> borious keeping of the law, his struggles and victories, were in a moment set in a new light, devalued, the merest ABC of moral attainment, beside the demand of Jesus to "sell all . . . and give . . . Come . . . follow me!" It was no more than Peter, John, and the rest had done; but it implied yielding up control, and consecration, and commitment. And it seemed too much.
>
> . . . Jesus had presented the towering moral challenge of His gospel—devotion to the good of others, denial of the claims of self, dedication to the will of God. Knowing himself unwilling, yet realizing that such was indeed the way to life eternal, the young man turned sadly away, humbled, chastened, self-exposed.
>
> And Jesus let him go.[9]

The conditions of discipleship must never be understood as a moral code that Jesus demanded from only a few. All who would follow Christ and be His disciples must meet the same conditions. There can be no exceptions.

Cost of Discipleship. Men did not follow Jesus blindly. He told them what it would cost to be His disciple. Jesus invited men to come and to take up His yoke as a mark of discipleship. Those who desired to be disciples must count the cost. It was necessary to take these steps: (1) forsake all, (2) deny self, (3) take up the cross, and (4) follow Christ.

Let's take a look at these steps:

(1) *Forsake All.* Jesus declared that those who would not forsake everything could not be His disciples. All conflicting loyalties must be put aside. He said exactly the same things about salvation and discipleship. The

---

[9] White, *op. cit.,* p. 72. Used by permission.

young rich ruler was told to ". . . sell all . . . Come . . . follow me." Nothing less than complete dedication was sufficient. When Jesus insisted that a man must "hate" his family, friends and possessions, He did not mean that men should despise these things.[10] Jesus wanted men to have the love of a family, share the joy of friendship, and possess sufficient earthly goods to insure a happy life, but He did not want these things to stand between Him and the disciples. He demanded priority. Jesus was comparing human love to the new spiritual love the disciple would have for the heavenly Father. Compared to the human emotion and physical attachment the spiritual love of the disciple was to be so great that all else seemed as hate. However, there are cases in which men must literally forsake all earthly attachments to assure a proper attachment to Christ, but in such cases the disciple is promised "an hundredfold" reward in this life, and in the world to come he is promised eternal life.[11]

(2) *Deny Self*. Denying self is accepting Jesus Christ as Lord. This is a vital part of discipleship. Man must be "delivered from the body of this death." Selfish ambitions have no place in discipleship. The capital "I" in SIN is the source of most human difficulties. S. D. Gordon aptly expressed the idea when he said, "In every redeemed heart there is a throne and a cross. If self is on the throne, Jesus is on the cross . . . If self is your King, if self is on your throne, Jesus is on the cross. . . . Let self be on the cross and Jesus on the throne." Self must be crucified; Christ must rule and reign.

> In full and glad surrender,
> I give myself to Thee:
> Thine utterly and only
> And evermore to be.
> Oh, come and reign, Lord Jesus!

---

[10] Luke 14:26; Matthew 10:36-39.
[11] Matthew 19:29.

Rule over everything!
And keep me always loyal
And true to Thee, MY KING![12]

(3) *Take Up the Cross.* The disciple must be identified with Jesus Christ, and the cross is that identification. There is only one cross, the cross of Jesus Christ. This is the "yoke" of which Jesus spoke, the symbol of death, and the believer must be "crucified with Christ" to become His disciple. We should not sing, "Jesus, I my cross have taken . . . " in reality it is, "Jesus, I Thy cross have taken, all to leave and follow Thee." Taking up the cross is the disciple's way of saying "yes" to Christ and "no" to self and to the world which is the only way to be free from self. Until an individual is willing to take up the cross and to follow Jesus, he is not worthy to be a disciple.

(4) *Follow Christ.* Obeying the call of Jesus means following Jesus Christ. This must be the innermost longing of the soul. Following Christ includes a desire to know Him in the power of His resurrection and in the fellowship of His suffering. Following Christ causes the believer to be made conformable unto His death and makes him willing to take up His cross. Any who will not follow Christ and will not meet these conditions has no right to claim to be His disciple. Those who will not be a disciple have no reason to claim to be a Christian. The Christian must first be a disciple of Jesus Christ.

What does it mean to be a Christian? The disciples were first called Christians at Antioch. They were first of all disciples of Christ and, because of their association with Him and His way of life, they became known as Christians. This was to identify their relationship with Christ. It is tragic that many desire to be Christians but are not willing to pay the price of discipleship. These

---
12 Quoted by King, *op. cit.*, pp. 27, 28.

would-be disciples desire to reduce discipleship to the level of their lives and to stipulate their own terms.

There are three such would-be disciples spoken of in Luke's Gospel.[13]

The first would follow Jesus without waiting to be called, and Jesus warns him that he does not understand the meaning of discipleship. The disciple is called to a life of self-sacrifice and service. Without the call of Christ, the individual would not be able to pay the price. The second would-be disciple is called by Jesus to follow Him, but he wanted to bury his father first! At the critical moment when Jesus calls a man to follow Him nothing—not even the law itself—must act as a barrier to discipleship. The ones called must accept the absolute authority of Jesus and must follow Him without hesitation. The third would-be disciple was similar to the first who offered to follow Jesus on his own initiative, but this one was bold enough to stipulate his own terms. He was not willing to give Jesus priority. He placed a barrier between Christ and himself by wanting to go first and to bid farewell to his family and his friends. This was a normal thing to do, but Christ had called him and He demanded first place in that life. He wanted to follow, but he felt obliged to insist on his own terms. Discipleship to him was something that he could choose for himself at his time and at his place and at his price. This could never be Christian discipleship. These three men illustrate some of the basic problems of discipleship: hearing the call, forsaking all, denying self, counting the cost, and following Christ.

III. DISCIPLESHIP DEMANDED

The new discipline taught and lived by Jesus Christ demands discipleship and produces two practical problems.

---
[13] Luke 9:57-62.

First, one must apply the new discipline to his life; second, he should find the power to accept and to put the demands into action. These are man's most urgent and most practical problems. Discipleship is demanded by Jesus Christ, and it requires a decision to follow Him.

When Christ calls a man to follow Him, He expects the person to apply the new discipline to his life. Jesus Christ is the same and the requirements of discipleship have not changed. He still requires an exceeding righteousness. When a man is called to discipleship, Christ Himself furnishes the strength to follow. He manifested amazing confidence in average men and committed into their hands the work of the Kingdom. Jesus seemed to have unwavering confidence in the men who had accepted His discipline. He was certain that the growing power of His teaching on their lives and deeds would be sufficient to produce disciples of distinction for the Kingdom.

The objective of the Great Commission is the making of disciples. God has been throughout the history of man in the process of teaching men, of making disciples, and of creating His glorious likeness within them. It is through these means that He is preparing them for a new world order designated as His Kingdom. God expects the followers of Christ to be busy in the world, making disciples by precept and practice.

The foundation and the function of the mighty movement established on earth by Jesus Christ before His return to the Father is adequately described in these words of J. Clyde Yates:

> The foundation was laid deep and strong by Jesus Christ in His marvelous ministry, His supreme sacrifice and His regnant resurrection. On the day of Pentecost the power of the Holy Spirit was poured out upon those dedicated disciples in abundant measure and might. Under

the impact and inspiration of His pervading presence, they went forth winning veritable and vital victories in the name of Jesus Christ. So mighty and majestic was the onward march of the Spirit-filled witnesses of the master, that their foes were baffled and beaten in all their attempts to stop them. Finally they said to Peter and those who were fellow-witnesses with him, "You must not speak any more in the name of Jesus." But the emboldened Apostles answered, "Whether it be right in the sight of God to hearken unto you more than unto God, judge ye. For we cannot but speak the things that we have heard and seen." There is an inward fire which cannot be quenched and an inner voice which cannot be stilled. They had a message that was too good to keep, that must be made known. They have salvation that must be shared, a light they must let shine. They knew a name that must be exalted, a Prince who must be crowned King of Kings and Lord of Lords.[14]

Why are many churches impotent and powerless— growing numerically, but failing to grow spiritually and at times not growing at all? Why do some churches fight a losing battle? Does the Gospel have no power to transform lives and to transfer the interests of men from themselves to Jesus Christ? Is God different from what He was in the days of the Apostles? Does Jesus no longer call man to follow Him? Was God more concerned about the Early Church than He is the churches today? The answer to all these questions is an emphatic "no." The church has failed to lift up Jesus Christ as the real Saviour and Lord of men's lives. The claims of discipleship have not been placed before the people who profess

---
14 Yates, *loc. cit.*

Christ. The church has secured only decisions and has stopped short of making disciples. Christian discipleship is still possible and Jesus Christ still demands it.

What is a Christian? What is a disciple? A believer who learns the doctrine and discipline of Jesus Christ and whose life is changed by His power is a Christian. A believer who desires to live close to God and who follows Christ daily and devotes himself to a life of truth and is committed to the principle of right is a disciple. The call, "Follow Me" was not made to the Twelve alone, but to each man who lives. Jesus Christ demands decision; He demands discipleship. Each man is challenged to decide about Jesus Christ and the discipline of His Kingdom. A choice must be made: it is discipleship or disaster.

DISCUSSION GUIDE

1. What is discipleship?

2. How are salvation and discipleship related?

3. What does it mean to be a Christian?

4. Why are some churches powerless today? How can this be changed?

5. What does it mean to "deny self"?

Chapter Four

DECALOGUE OF DUTY

There is no attempt in this section to present solutions to particular moral problems or to dictate in detail the behavior appropriate to every circumstance of life. Instead, an effort is made to set forth certain basic obligations that must be remembered and to which conduct must conform if it is to be considered Christian.

The Bible itself does not give man a detailed list of specified rules of conduct. The Christian life is learned primarily from the way Christians live. It is taught by example, but the examples could not possibly cover every situation of life. In the Gospels and Acts, the foundation of Christian doctrine is begun and afterwards is elaborated in the Epistles and is exemplified in the lives of the early believers. The Bible, however, gives man a basic formula to assure his proper conduct: Jesus Christ is to work a work in the heart of man, to change his nature, and to motivate his life; the Holy Ghost is to guide the believer in developing a mature personality and to direct his daily life and conduct.

The problems of the times must be dealt with constructively. A creative initiative must be brought to the task of Christian living, based on the words and deeds of Jesus Christ and empowered by the guiding force of the Holy Spirit. Jesus Christ is alive today. The Holy Spirit is in the world to guide men into all truth. These facts make Christians aware that they are not enslaved by a written code. Equally they are not left to their own devices. Believers are living under the discipline of the church and the rule of Jesus Christ. Jesus is adequate for all their needs. Before men is the divine record: the teachings of Jesus Christ, the history of the Early Church, and the examples of Christian men. It is clear from these that the strongest force for right living is still Jesus Christ. Believers have the assurance of His direct aid through the Spirit as they seek to understand and to apply the will of God to their affairs. Christ still leads the way. More than that, He gives us the strength to follow Him.

Christian Obligation

The basic obligation of Christian discipleship is that of making Christianity visible, intelligible, and desirable. Christian disciples are to show that their viewpoint is practical, that the Christian concept of life makes sense, and that the Christian faith is satisfying and relevant. There is no discipleship unless everything is staked on what is believed. The disciple must *live* the gospel he believes. A theology not based on experience and testimony cannot be Christian.

The life of a Christian disciple should enable the world to see more clearly the working of divine grace and glory of God manifest in a transformed life. The arena of Christian service and the circumstance of each life are different, but the basic pattern of discipleship and spiritual activity is the same. Each life must manifest the work of the Master Teacher in daily deed and devotion.

Discipleship is an interpersonal relationship between God and man, and it is of value in marking this individual and his personal relationship. It should be remembered that Jesus Himself used the term and even

DECALOGUE OF DUTY

the angel with the resurrection message said, "Go tell His disciples." The term is also used in the Book of Acts; however, the specific designation of the Twelve as *His disciples* later gave way to the use of the word *Christian*. It is noteworthy that the word *disciple* cannot be found in the epistles. Why was this? Was discipleship so soon to be a thing of the past?

The Early Church was not far removed from the days of Jesus Christ and the vital facts of discipleship. The life of Paul is a good example of discipleship. The full price of discipleship was demanded even to be associated with the Christian cause in the early days of the church. Most of the epistles were directed to the brethren, the saints, the believers, in their corporate capacity as churches, but discipleship is a personal matter. The writers of the epistles were concerned with the edification of the total body of believers, but this edification was to come from the personal improvement of each believer in his devotion to Christ and His way of life. This is discipleship! The first Christians had no New Testament. They worked out their personal problems of faith and conduct under the inspiration of their immediate sense of discipleship to Jesus and through the guidance of the Holy Ghost.

The Christian Ideal

The Christian ideal lies before every believer, not as a remote mountain peak, but as an ethical Everest which must be scaled by individual skill and endurance. This ideal is a narrow path on which man may walk with Christ, guided by the Holy Ghost, and assured of constant companionship.

The life and discipline of Jesus Christ will have constructive consequences on the behavior of believers. He is the only adequate motivation to right living. Jesus Christ is the dynamic force of discipleship. Mere legalism cannot produce true disciples or Christian conduct. Jesus never intended for the Sermon on the Mount to be made into a new Pharisaism. Such legalism emphasized the less important issues of life and ignored the weighty matters. It often bypasses such sins as pride, anger, or envy and gives the impression that the Christian life is one of staying out of trouble.

The Christian life is more than negative living; it is positive virtue flowing out of the regenerate core of the heart of man. Sanctification is more than mere abstinence, it is the Lordship of Christ and the rule of the Spirit. It issues in love, kindness and compassion and good works humbly done. Therefore, there can be no detailed regulation of daily situations. The principle force of right must be in the heart. Mere mechanical imitation of Christ cannot produce discipleship. Christians are not sheer imitators of Christ; they are partakers of His divine nature. Believers are "sons of God," "joint heirs with Christ," and they participate in the work of God in the world. Peter uttered a universal prayer when he asked that men "might be partakers of the divine nature."[1] Man has a capacity within his nature for the likeness of God. It is possible to be so united and related to Christ that His strength becomes the believer's strength for daily living.[2]

Believers must not shrink from the Christian ideal. They must have the consecration, the dedication, and the determination to become the person they know they ought to be. If Christianity is to have meaning, it must prove itself as a force by which men can live, and in which they can find re-enforcement and support, not only in the secret chamber, but in the performance of their daily tasks in the work-a-day world.

The individual believer must realize that his respon-

---

[1] 2 Peter 1:4.
[2] Leonard H. Cochran, *Man at his Best*. (New York: Abingdon Press, 1957), p. 90.

sibility is to contribute to the total Christian witness. The basic problem involved in making this contribution seems to be that of how Christians are to live and act in the various relationships of life. The believer is a new man, a citizen of a new Kingdom, but he lives in the world and must constantly associate with both the brethren of the faith and the men of the world. Earnest believers are asking disturbing questions about their responsibilities. What should the Christian's response be toward the enormous pressures and intimidations of the world?

The principles of discipleship must be applied by the individual to his daily life. This is often a difficult task, because it speaks of *duty* which word has some objections. In popular usage the word *duty* carries the thought of strain or constrain; however, Christian duty should be a delight. Doing one's duty should be regarded as a privilege rather than a burden. Love of the right and of the good can transform the whole idea of moral obligation, making duty a delight. Those who perform duties with sincerity and willingness transform their obligations into victories and afterwards feel the "answer of a good conscience toward both God and man."

It is true that man's destiny lies beyond this life and that this world of probation is to prepare man for the hereafter. Yet Christianity is intensively practical, touching the daily life of man at every point. The first part of this book was concerned primarily with man's chief responsibility—fellowship with God. Attempts were made to answer these questions: How can the broken relationship between God and man be restored? How can reconciliation be effected, and on what basis can man be acceptable in the sight of God? Finding a way to God and living in constant communion with Jesus Christ has been the basic objective to this point, even though certain aspects of the Christian's relationship with others was discussed. Now the concern is with the believer's daily life as a result of this fellowship with Jesus Christ. What influence does it have on his affairs with men? What is the effect of discipleship on the common relationships of life?

Consider the ten basic obligations of man: duty to God, to self, to family, to church, to brethren, to neighbor, to enemy, to sinner, to state and to the world.

I. DUTY TO GOD

The whole duty of man is summarized in his duty to God. All obligations are duties to God. Man's duties to himself and to his fellow men blend and overlap and are a part of his obligation to God. The very essence of man's spiritual obligation is summed up in Ecclesiastes: (1) Fear God, and (2) keep His commandments.[3] The "fear of God" is the definition of true religion in the Old Testament and means a reverence and trust in God combined with a hatred of all that is evil. It is the beginning of wisdom, the secret of uprightness, and the distinguishing factor of the people who give God pleasure.[4] It causes men to keep God's commandments. The prophet Micah gave these words on the subject of religious responsibility: "He has shewed thee, O man, what is good; and what doth the Lord require of thee but to do justly, and to love mercy, and to walk humbly with thy God?"[5]

The primary duty of man is to God. He must (1) recognize God as the Eternal Father, (2) obey and serve God, and (3) worship and trust God. The commandment of primary obligation is in both the Old and the New Testaments.[6] The first commandment is to

---
[3] Ecclesiastes 12:13.
[4] Psalm 111:10; Proverbs 8:13; Psalm 147:11.
[5] Micah 6:8.
[6] Deuteronomy 6:5; Matthew 22:37, 38.

"love the Lord thy God . . ." This principle of primary obligation is taught by Jesus Christ and the Apostle Paul.[7]

Recognize God

The Bible presupposes God's eternal existence and, therefore, makes no effort to prove its truth. However, there is ample evidence to convince the inquiring mind that there is an eternal Deity. Being convinced of God's existence is an act of faith, but once man musters this faith it logically follows that man must recognize God in the affairs of his life.

Man's recognition of God, the Eternal Father, can be illustrated by the father-son relationship. No man could live in his father's house and not recognize the paternal interests and care. A worthy son would not eat at his father's table, share his bounty, and then ignore the father day after day by never speaking, nor showing any sign of appreciation to him. When the father is recognized for his paternal care, he will be honored and revered by the faithful son. There will be love, gratitude, and devotion to motivate the son's affection toward the father. These facts can easily be applied to man's relationship with God.[8]

When man recognizes God, as the Eternal Father, reverence, respect, and repentence are logical consequences. Confronted by the power and holiness of God, man is "naked" and aware of his sinfulness. This awareness of sin brings about godly sorrow and a humble request for God's intervention into man's affairs. This divine intervention comes by faith and brings man salvation. And with salvation comes an anticipation of eternal fellowship with God.

---

[7] Matthew 6:33; 1 Corinthians 10:31.
[8] Leander S. Keyser, *A System of General Ethics*. (Burlington, Iowa: The Lutheran Literary Board, 1954), p. 227.

Obey and Serve God

Aware of the knowledge of sins forgiven, man must actively seek the will of God, and, once he knows this will, joyously do it. God reveals His will to obedient hearts. As the believer walks the way of obedience, he discovers that doing the will of God is best for all concerned. When a man obeys God, he commits himself to do God's will. This conception of obedience means that the divine will becomes an active, dynamic force in one's life. It is clear that obedience implies service to God.

The power to discharge the obligations of life and to do spiritual service does not lie within the individual. No amount of education, training, or experience can adequately suffice to enable man to give God, himself, or others that which is the divine requirement. These things will most assuredly help, but they are not sufficient within themselves. There is no spiritual power in the flesh. The secret of spiritual service is in the willingness of man to obey God. A man can live a righteous life and discharge his moral duties when he lives a life of obedience to the will of God.

Man can do nothing to put himself in right relationship with God. Rather, the grace of God must be the starting point. He must live his life from God outward. There must be an earnestness toward God that seeks guidance and help. When these are present in the heart of man, the duties to God are no more a terrifying demand. They become the rule of life which the believer embraces with devotion and delight.

Worship and Trust God

Obeying and serving God naturally leads one to the worship of God. Man must see that every area of his life honors God and is within the divine will and purpose. Walking sincerely before God in an attitude of worship is essential to doing God's will and enjoying spiritual health. God is adored and exaulted by a consistent life of devotion, pure thoughts and prayer, systematic Bible reading, sincere meditation and service, public worship, and serious daily living.

Worship involves trusting God. The disciples of Jesus were taught to pray: "Thy will be done."[9] Trusting God is inherently beautiful and something seems basically wrong about a man's refusing to trust Him. A man who worships the eternal God should be able to defend the faith with confidence, bear the chastisements of God without murmering, and rejoice in the hope of eternal fellowship with Him.

II. DUTY TO SELF

Many would prefer the order of God, others, and self. The fact that self is placed second in treatment is deliberate. Duty to God involves obligations to self and to others, but man cannot fulfill his spiritual obligation to others until he has first established a proper relationship with the eternal God. The basic obligation of man is to give himself to God and to be concerned about his own spiritual welfare. Then, with this connection firmly established, he will be adequately prepared to take care of the spiritual needs of his family and friends. This admonition is definite: "Take heed unto thyself."[10]

Self-Respect

The fact that man is the foremost of God's creation implies that God put the divine impress upon each individual so that each person has intrinsic worth. Each man must see his own worth. The dignity of man is expressed in his divine origin, his upright position, his

---
9 Matthew 6:10.
10 2 Timothy 4:16; 1 Corinthians 11:28; 2 Corinthians 13:5.

graceful form and movement, and in the fact that he can possess inner character that guides his life.[11] The body of man houses a spiritual being that is eternal. This soul is worth more than the world. This fact should give each man a certain degree of self-respect and cause him to regard himself as an individual who is capable of accomplishments under God's direction.

Self-Development

The capacity and capabilities given to man by God require him to develop and to improve himself. There are four basic areas of self-development: mental, physical, spiritual, and social. The knowledge that Jesus had a fourfold development—mental, physical, spiritual, and social—should be sufficient impetus for the believer's self-improvement.[12]

1. *Mental.* The Christian is encouraged to develop his mental powers. The capacity for learning is a gift from God and should be used f o r God's glory. Consecrated brain power can mean the difference between success and failure in this enlightened age. The Bible warns that men will learn, but that they never come to the full knowledge of the truth. It is evident, then, that man should carefully choose the facts to be learned. The believer is obligated to develop his mind to the best advantage of God's cause in the world.[13] The development should come in at least these areas:

    (a) Basic knowledge.
    (b) Understanding.
    (c) Memory and reflection.
    (d) Power of the will.

2. *Physical.* Living in the body that God has given

---
[11] Keyser, *op. cit.,* p. 154.
[12] Luke 2:52.
[13] 2 Timothy 2:15; 1 Timothy 4:13

him, man becomes conscious of the world of creation. He has the capacity to learn to control and to regulate the body in which he lives. It should be pointed out that no natural passion or appetite is wrong of its own nature. They are given for good and useful purposes in the life of man. However, the perversion and abuse of any physical appetite is grossly sinful and injurious to both man's physical and spiritual nature and, therefore, unnatural usage of any of these desires must be condemned. Nature herself seems to place a stamp of approval on the moderate and orderly use of natural forces. Man is told to "glorify God in his body," because it is God's.[14]

The physical house of man is a marvelous mechanism of divine origin, made for a wise and noble purpose— to glorify God the Creator. Man's body is superior to all other organisms of the earth and should have respect and dignity. The Christian understanding is that the body is to be "the temple of the Holy Ghost." The body of itself is not evil and must not be viewed as the seat of defilement. Sin is the source of evil in the universe and the body is evil only when it is an instrument of sin. The Christian, however, believes that the blood of Jesus Christ can redeem man from the curse of sin and make the "vilest sinner clean."

Man has an obligation to preserve his physical health. Anointed physical health can become spiritual energy and man-power consecrated and harnessed by God becomes the force that moves the world toward God. Here are four ways to preserve physical health:

    (a) Cleanliness of body and mind.
    (b) Proper food and drink.
    (c) Adequate physical exercise (work and play).
    (d) Proper rest and relaxation.

3. *Spiritual.* The believer is required to learn of Jesus

---
[14] 1 Corinthians 6:19, 20.

Christ and to grow in "grace and knowledge." The physical, mental, and social areas of self-development relate directly to the spiritual. They are considered because of this relationship. It is evident that a stronger body, a better developed mental capacity, and harmonious social relations can contribute to the well-being of the spiritual man. It is also true that a properly developed spiritual life will affect the individual's health, mental attitude, and social life.

4. *Social.* Man is by nature a social creature, and he is obligated to develop this part of his life. An effort must be made to live in harmony with all men. The social side of man's development may seem contrary to his spiritual life. This is not necessarily true. It depends on which is developed first. Provided the example of Jesus is followed—mental, physical, spiritual and then the social development—the social area can be an asset to the Christian life. To care adequately for the social needs, the individual must first have a proper development of the mind, body, and the spiritual life. The spiritual life will produce harmonious social relations. Jesus Christ was the friend of sinners, but this friendship had a spiritual motivation. (More on the subject of man's relation with man can be found in Part One, Chapter III.)

There must be a *balance* among these areas of self-development. In the physical there must be a balance between work and rest: neither must suffer at the expense of the other. The mental development should have a balance between study, or gathering knowledge, and the use of truth in life and service. In the area of social development, the balance must be between perfecting one's personality and the cultivation of friendship with others. This self-development and social improvement must then be used to the spiritual advantage of all concerned. In the realm of the spiritual, there ought to be a balance between profession and practice. The spiritual development should be such as would bring about balance between such contrasting elements as firmness and kindness, faith and works, worship and service, hearing and doing. The spiritual life must first be motivated by New Testament principles and Christian consideration of self and others from which the practical and proper action will issue spontaneously.

Self-Preservation

There is a physical and a spiritual law of self-preservation. This is a law that preserves oneself from destruction, injury, and loss. In the physical realm this law seems to be an instinct or a natural law common to all men, but in the spiritual an awareness of this law must be developed. Man has the basic capacity for a spiritual law of self-preservation, but for it to be useful to his spiritual life he must diligently cultivate a proper spiritual attitude of himself and his spiritual nature.

The spiritual law is developed from the basic obligation of priority that the Christian must give to the Kingdom. It produces a desire to protect one's spiritual nature from injury, loss or ultimate destruction by the forces of evil. This spiritual law, once it is cultivated in the heart, will cause man to set aside anything that disrupts his communion with God or weakens his appetite for the Word of God, or dilutes his desire for spiritual worship, or dulls his concern for the welfare of himself or others.

Man must remember to take heed to himself first. He has an obligation to his own spiritual life. Salvation and discipleship are personal matters between man and God, and nothing should be allowed to interfere with man's personal relationship with God.

III. DUTY TO THE FAMILY

The family is a divine institution, but it is not exclusively a Christian one. The family unit can be found in all cultures, but the Christian experience and the Christian way of life have made the family a Christian institution.

Christian Marriage

Marriage is a holy institution resting on divine ordinance and will.[15] The Christian concept of marriage is a strict monogamy based on the existence of genuine personal love and a mutual desire to live together permanently in the enjoyment of this love. The divine ideal is one man and one woman for life. Christian marriage is considered an honorable safeguard against immorality and a proper means of propagating the race. The permanence of Christian marriage between two people is based on a moral purpose and never on physical attraction.[16] Marriage is a venture into a new kind of life. There are risks and inevitable disillusionment, but when two people agree in love to live for Christ, they can receive strength to solve the daily problems.

The church is a powerful re-enforcement to the true meaning of Christian marriage.[17] For this reason, the wedding vows should be repeated in the church before a minister. A Christian marriage takes for granted that both the husband and the wife will actively participate in the spiritual life of the church. It is clear that marriage should be between persons of similar religious convictions.[18] Failure on the part of the contracting parties to live up to this expectation will have grave consequences. "Can two walk together, except they be agreed?"

---

[15] Genesis 1:27, 28; 2:18.

[16] Matthew 19:3-6.

[17] Titus 2:4-8. Even love needs training and discipline to be wisely expressed.

[18] 2 Corinthians 6:14.

Christian Home

Christian marriage is expected to establish a Christian home into which children will be born, loved, and brought up in the fear and the admonition of the Lord. The New Testament presents the ideal Christian home and implies that the whole of man's human relationships are to be influenced by Jesus Christ.

Christ Claims Authority. Jesus Christ claims absolute supremacy over all life. He must have authority in the Christian home. The initial requirements of discipleship cannot be abandoned. Jesus Christ must motivate the family life. The obligation of believers to any person is limited or enforced by his supreme obligation to Jesus Christ. This obligation is greater than that of wife to husband, child to parent, or servant to master. All harmonious relationships in these areas are approved by Jesus, but He claims first place in the heart of the believer. Nothing must come between Jesus Christ and those who follow Him. Contrary to the thinking of some persons there can be no two people closer in human love than those who have both given themselves completely to Jesus Christ. This is the secret of supreme happiness in the Christian home.

Christian Attitude. The Christian experience creates a Christian attitude toward others and governs the relationship of each member of the family to the other members. Once a self has been committed to God it can never be pre-eminent; God is first and having placed His love within the believer's heart, there will be a Christian attitude toward others. When each member of the family recognizes Jesus Christ as the supreme Being, they will find their relationship toward each other ennobled and purified as they enjoy the multiplied blessings of a Christian home.

A most glorious picture of the Christian home is presented in the writings of the Apostle Paul, a man who for the cause of Christ gave up the joys of such a life. However, it is evident that Paul understood the simplicity and the beauty of the Christian home. He was primarily concerned with the Christian life within the family institution, and he pictured this ideal.

Christian Family Relationships

A general introduction to the subject of family relationship is given in these words of Paul: "And whatsoever ye do in word or deed, do all in the name of the Lord Jesus, g i v i n g thanks to God and the F a t h e r by him."[19] He believed that to relate oneself to another "in the name of Jesus," meant to do so "in His power" or "as belonging to Him." Even simple family relationships are to be determined on the basis of the believer's belonging to Christ.

A table of duties for the members of the family appear in Paul's writings.[20] He places emphasis on order, obedience, subordination, and respect for authority. His comments on the Christian family relationship seem to be an elaboration on the fact that the Christian life is lived in the midst of the common duties of life.

Husband and Wife. The relationship between husband and wife is a figure of the relationship between Christ and the church. The ideal of true love is expressed in Ephesians: "Husbands, love your wives, even as Christ also loved the church, . . . " The order of things by virtue of creation would suggest that the wife was to be subject to her husband. This does not mean being in bondage. Paul is careful to make certain that the subjection of wife to husband is regulated by the Christian formula: "in the Lord." When the husband loves with the love

---

[19] Colossians 3:17.
[20] Colossians 3:18-4:1; Ephesians 5:21-6:9.

DECALOGUE OF DUTY

of Christ, the wife's love is realized and finds its highest manifestation in submission.

The husband—wife relationship is to be maintained until the death of one of the partners, except in extreme circumstances.[21] Even in marriages consummated before conversion, the believer is to make fervent effort to convert the other partner to the faith and thus establish a Christian home.[22] All the problems of the married life are to be settled by the force of the partner's personal Christian faith. "Dwell . . . giving honor . . . as being heirs together of the grace of life; that your prayers be not hindered."[23]

Paul presented the ideal, but discipleship is often maintained in very different circumstances. At times there is only one who serves Christ and the ideal home situation is marred by this division. The position of the disciple in such a case is indeed difficult, but the grace of God is sufficient. (See figure 3, p. 43.)

Responsibility of Parents. There must be a joint assumption of certain responsibilities in marriage. The husband and wife, as parents, have responsibilities to their children. The paternal responsibility is clearly stated in Paul's words: "And, ye fathers, provoke not your children to wrath: but bring them up in the nurture and admonition of the Lord." Children are to be tenderly trained and disciplined in a manner so as not to gender resentment to the parents' authority. "Train up a child," best expresses the individual responsibility of the parent to each child.

The greatest contribution any parent can make to his child's life is to bring that child into a vital faith in Jesus Christ. Greater than fame and better than fortune, even more important than education is the giving to

---

[21] Matthew 5:31, 32.
[22] 1 Corinthians 7:10-16; 1 Peter 3:1-5.
[23] 1 Peter 3:7.

each child the gift of faith. It will be enlarged as the child grows and all of his life will be sweeter, stronger, and better for having had faith in God.

Children learn from their parents characteristic attitudes toward life. The family is the most important realm of social and Christian education. The best methods by which the parents can teach is by *precept* and by *practice*. Children learn to love, trust, and obey Jesus Christ when He is the Lord in the lives of their parents. A great percentage of what children learn comes from the parents' example. If they learn to pray, it is from seeing the parents pray. If they learn to read the Bible, it is from hearing it read to them. Children who are "sent to church" while their parents remain at home do not receive the full benefit of the worship. The influence and benefit of the church is best exerted when church becomes a family affair.

The religious responsibility of parents includes: family Bible reading and prayer, regular public worship, and consistent Christian living. The whole family ought to attend the church services together and readily discuss the spiritual truth learned and the blessings experienced. The abandonment of these age-old customs is a tragic reality in many modern homes and the result can only be determined by time and eternity.

Child and Parent. This is a very tender and intimate relationship and is to be one of obedience "in the Lord." This God-created relationship is so grand and glorious until it is usually not properly appreciated until it has passed. The beauty of a tender child influenced by a godly parent is portrayed throughout the Bible. Jesus was displeased with anyone who refused to take time to help children enter the Kingdom. He declared that children belonged in His Kingdom.[24]

The child is to learn obedience to his parents as prepa-

---

24 Luke 18:15-17.

ration for his obeying the divine will in his later life. Any child who does not learn to respect parental authority will not be likely to respect authority of any kind—CIVIL OR DIVINE.

Church and Home

There are four fundamentally important institutions: home, school, church, and the state. Each has a distinct contribution to make to the social order of man. However, the church and the home are most important from the Christian standpoint.

The home is the oldest and most basic of these institutions, and it molds the lives of children before school, church, and state exert extensive influence on them. For this reason, it is most important. The home is of paramount importance in the life of man. No Christian service that is contradicted by the life at home is of much value. Modern man often neglects the home for multiplied engagements. This seems to be the spirit of the times.

The home of the Christian should be conducive to spiritual progress. The Bible is explicit that the Christian home is the practical center for the teaching of religion. The home has first and foremost influence in the life of the child. It is there that he is best understood and most loved. The Christian home gives opportunity for worship, education, discipline, Christian example and leadership. Life's basic concepts are determined in the home by clear teaching of the Bible, the example of godly parents and the loving atmosphere of Christian fellowship.

The church was established to aid the home in its high function. Here the family worships together and is ministered to from the Word of God. The home is no longer the center of family activity. A child is born in a hospital, fed out of a bottle, raised in a nursery, clothed by a factory, schooled by the public, entertained by the crowd, and often neglected by the parents. The home is sacred, but little provision is made for the spiritual well-being of the modern family. The busy world leaves little time for parents to prepare themselves or their families to face life's problems.

The church must assume an active role in the preparation of the family for life and death. The church must guide the parents through the educational program and the regular worship services. The family and the home must be a vital part of the total ministry of the church.

IV. DUTY TO THE CHURCH

The life of Jesus Christ and the work of His Church is the force of the Christian faith today. Jesus Christ had an eternal effect on the lives and deeds of men. They forsook all, denied themselves, took up the cross, and followed Him to their very death. Not only what Jesus began to do and to teach in the Gospels changed the lives of men, but what He continued to do and to teach through His Church. Consecrated, Spirit-filled lives of the Early Church transformed men into Christian disciples.

Everything dear to the heart of Jesus Christ is tied up in the church and its work in the world. The New Testament knew nothing of "free lance" Christianity. The believers were united for personal edification and Christian witness. The church was a "fellowship" of all who found union with God, and who would bring the reality of Jesus Christ into all their living. A holy love bound them together as a resolute band of believers determined to change the world for Christ.

The church ministered to the various needs of the individual for personal edification and each believer contributed to the effectiveness of the total Christian witness. Exerting Christian influence was the result of the united effort of all believers to live for Jesus Christ in the world. To accomplish this influence, each believer had to maintain his personal experience with Christ.

The purpose of the church is to maintain Christian ideals, to edify believers, to reach the lost, and to be a Christian influence in the world. The church is weak today despite numerical strength, because men often expect the corporate image of the church to be sufficient Christian influence on the world. The church cannot do the task that has been assigned to the individual Christian. Nothing effectively can be done so long as the church is thought of as a whole. Practical thinking is personal. The church is only the aggregate of all its members and cannot be better than the spiritual experience of those who compose it.

It is a fallacy to reason that what is true of the whole is true of the part.[25] The church with all its purity and power can never by published standards alone influence the world. The faith and the Christian standards of the church must be exemplified in the lives of individuals. Discipleship is an individual matter just as salvation is a personal experience. Christ is the Builder of the church, and it is true that the church contributes to the Christian life of man, but the world is influenced by the personal experience and testimony of believers. The individual Christian is a vital part of the church, but the Christian witness of the church is determined by how the individual members conduct themselves in their affairs with men.

Church Membership

The Christian must seek to understand the ministry of the church, its place and purpose in his life, and to

---

[25] Irving M. Copi, "The Fallacy of Division," *Introduction To Logic.* (New York: The MacMilian Co., 1953) pp. 75, 76.

attach himself to it with intelligence and loyalty as an earnest member. The duty of the Christian to belong to the church is involved in his duty to: Christ, himself, his fellow Christians, and the world. Membership in the church enlightens the believer of his Christian obligation and gives him strength to fulfill this duty.

The believer must not only be attached to Christ; there must also be a union with other believers. The abiding influence of the church is essential to maintain the proper relationship with God. The Bible clearly teaches that the Christian experience is strengthened by Christian fellowship and weakened by the lack of it. An alliance with other believers in the worship and work of the church assures continued fellowship with Christ.

Church membership is limited to those who meet certain requirements set forth in the Word of God. Anyone who does not meet the qualifications of personal salvation and a willingness to walk in the light of the Scripture cannot become a member of God's Church. Church membership, however, is a logical step for the converted person. His love and devotion to Jesus Christ will naturally cause him to associate with others who share the same attachment. The church is that divine institution that Jesus loved and sacrificed Himself to establish. It has a holy mission and a sacred message. It is natural for the followers of Christ to love the church and to desire its fellowship.

There is no security for the believer outside the protection and influence of the Christian fellowship. God's plan did not leave the convert to face the "wiles of the devil" alone. The church was established to provide a place of divine refuge and is the believer's God-given home. Membership in this chosen institution is important. Through the Word of God and constant Christian companionship, the believer gains strength and courage to meet life's most trying times. Every convert to the Christian faith belongs within this great company of believers. The spiritual life is impaired when fellowship with the church is lacking. Our Christian experience could not long exist in these last days without our participation in this vital part of God's plan.

Consistent Worship

Being a member of the church involves attendance at worship services and full participation in the life of the church with thankfulness in the heart to God. Membership responsibilities includes: being faithful to God, living a clean Christian life, remaining loyal and steadfast in faith, doing Christian service, assembling together, and encouraging one another.[26] Participation in such spiritual activity should bring the member into the very presence of God.

In the Creation God gave man a mind with which to think, a heart with which to love, a will with which to choose, and a soul which would be desirous of worship of God. Of all His creation, man alone possesses the capacity and desire to worship God. Worship is that necessary nourishment and pleasure the spiritual man needs to grow in grace. Man can worship God anywhere at anytime, but generally he worships best in groups.[27] The individual who fails to participate in public worship usually will not have the desire or the strength to maintain family worship or personal meditation and prayer.

The believer has an obligation to God, himself, his family, and the church to be consistent in public worship. Active participation in the life of the church is necessary to keep membership meaningful. Without regular atten-

---

[26] Colossians 3:15, 16.

[27] Group activity becomes less satisfying as the group becomes larger. To survive, large churches must have many small groups active in the life of the church: strong family emphasis, effective Sunday School classes, prayer groups, study groups, youth groups, fellowship groups, and other such groups and activities.

dance interest will decline and the Christian unity of the believer with others will be dissolved. When the frequency of attendance and participation decreases, a decrease in the strength of the fellowship will follow. As a result, members seem to become "neutral" in their feelings to one another. Even when the Early Church was meeting almost daily, the writer of Hebrews warned against "forsaking the assembling of ourselves together." An additional injunction followed: "And so much the more as ye see the day approaching." If this has meaning for today, no mere once a week gathering will suffice to keep the worship of God and the vital fellowship of the church alive.[28]

Worship must be the motivating force of church attendance. A Christian test of worship causes the believer to ask: "Does my church attendance make me more Christlike in attitude and behavior?" Church attendance or merely being a spectator at a worship service is not enough. Church attendance must be used for the true worship of God and should never become a substitute for worship. Worship ought to re-enforce the believer's Christian behavior. This is suggested when Jesus talks of a man who brings his gift to the altar and remembers that he and his brother are in disagreement. Jesus declared that this worshiper must first be reconciled to his fellow men and then his worship would have meaning, and God would receive his gift at the altar.[29]

Cheerful Support

God has ordained that the church should be supported and sustained by the moral and material interests of its membership. God's principle of personal, regular, freewill, cheerful giving is clearly set forth in the Bible. Christian giving is not a matter of law, but rather of

---
[28] Miller, *op. cit.*, p. 124.
[29] Matthew 5:23, 24.

grace. The supreme illustration of liberality is the sacrificial offering of Jesus Christ on the cross. Once the believer catches the spirit of Christian stewardship, his greatest joy is participating in the privilege of giving. The motivation is the spirit of Christ who gave His all.

Giving one-tenth to God's work was emphasized in the Old Testament. However, the law of the tithe has not been abolished or repealed. Tithe giving has been accepted in the New Testament as a lesson learned by example. This rule of giving has stood the test of time and experience. The Jews were blessed by their practice of tithing and this principle of giving has become the basis of the Christian's material obligation to the church.

An effective statement concerning tithing and giving was made by Dr. W. L. Prichard:

> Give the first tenth to the Lord. Use the next eight-tenths for the obligations of life. Save the last tenth and you will always have something for love offerings. Who ever follows this formula will have the high satisfaction of the respect of God and man.[30]

Consider a brief history of the tithe:

1. Abraham commenced it (Genesis 14:18-20).
2. Jacob continued it (Genesis 28:20-22).
3. Moses confirmed it (Leviticus 27:30-34).
4. Malachi commanded it (Malachi 3:10).
5. Jesus commended it (Luke 11:42).

When a Christian gives to support the church, he should give in the right spirit. It should be a privilege to give to the cause of Christ. All gifts should come from a heart of love. The story of the poor widow and

---

[30] To the student body at Mercer University.

her two mites tells of this full measure of devotion. She gave her all into the treasury of the Lord. Her gift was measured by what she had left and therefore her gift was considered greater than the gift of the rich men whose purses remained full.

A gift is measured in terms of the giver. It is not the size of the gift but the spirit of the giver that counts with God. A gift is measured by what it costs the giver. This sacrifice to the individual is a determining factor. Giving has been defined as "the unselfish outpouring of yourself in substance." It is the willing gift of one's possessions, with no return expected, that determines the measure of a gift and the reward of the giver.

A record of true love gifts to the work of the church is found in the Apostle Paul's counsel to the Corinthians to abound in the grace of liberality. Their example was the poor Macedonians who first gave themselves to God and then out of their deep poverty gave liberally to the work of God. The church would not want for support if all members followed Paul's advice: "Upon the first day of the week let everyone of you lay by him in store, as God hath prospered him." The Christian is obligated to regularly support the church in proportion to his prosperity.

Consider the Bible method of giving:

1. Without show (Matthew 6:3).
2. Regularly in proportion (1 Corinthians 16:2).
3. Cheerfully (2 Corinthians 9:7).
4. Liberally (Proverbs 11:25).
5. Sacrificially (2 Samuel 24:24).

The true spirit of worship creates in man a desire to give of himself and of his means to God in consecrated service. Participation increases one's inspiration for any effort. Those who know the most about God's work and participate fully in the activity of the church are the recipients of greater blessings and happiness.

Christian Living

The primary obligation of the believer to the church is that he live a Christian life and uphold the New Testament standard of Christianity. The Christian must take care to correlate his worship of God with the circumstances of everyday life. A re-enforcement for Christian living must come from worship, and Christian living should strengthen the desire for worship. If Christians are called to a life of holiness, it is because Jesus Christ has made it possible. Those who dare to believe can experience in their heart and demonstrate to others the reality of Christian living.

The consecrated Christian life is characterized by self-denial and complete devotion to the cause of Christ. Jesus Christ demanded discipleship and His church has the right to expect the believer to follow Christ daily. The Christian demonstrates his discipleship through his loyalty to the church. He must stand against wrong and stand for the right. He must live positively and seek to promote the principles of Christ through daily living.

The Christian is obligated to "walk worthy of God." When the Word of God is preached, the believer must receive and obey the Word. Notice these words of Paul:

> That ye would walk worthy of God, who hath called you unto his Kingdom and glory. For this cause also thank we God without ceasing, because, when ye received the word of God which ye heard of us, ye received it not as the word of men, but as it is in

truth, the word of God, which effectually worketh also in you that believe.[31]

When the believer worships God, he must let God speak directly to him. The Christian must lay aside all preconceived opinions and let the Word of God effectively work in his heart. When the Word does an effective work in the heart, the believer will go forth *living* the Word by life and lips. Believing is to help being. Doctrine is to make discipleship. Creed is to fashion character. Christian convictions constitute a call to be witnesses of the truth in life.

Christian Service

The church cannot fulfill its God-given task without believers whose lives have been changed and consecrated to Christian service. The church needs men who will outlive, outsuffer, and outwork the world and who will be a "burning and a shining light" for the Christian cause. The church should have unquestioned priority in the life of the Christian. Social and community activities, worthy as they may be, must take their chances with the remaining time.

Christian discipleship demands service. The believer must joyously search for God's will in a program of outgoing love and service. He should be busy in the service of the Lord. To live close to God, the believer must follow Christ in humble ways of Christian service.[32] He must stand in the presence of God, ready and willing to be sent to do God's work regardless of the circumstances.[33] Individuals have different abilities, but each Christian must employ his talents for the best interest of the Christian cause. Believers must work on joint

---

[31] 1 Thessalonians 2:12, 13.

[32] Dale Oldham, *Living Close to God*. (Anderson, Indiana: The Warner Press, 1957), p. 28.

[33] Luke 1:19. Gabriel is an example of absolute servitude.

projects in a united effort to advance their church and its ministry. Every area of man's life should be viewed as a prospective place for Christian service.

Christian service will cause the believer to participate in wholesome community activities, but this participation is always in his capacity as a Christian. He is a representative of his church, and he should endeavor to make his church so evidently a place of love and service that it would be greatfully welcomed in the life of the community. The dedicated Christian should pray for the opportunity and for the courage to infiltrate every segment of his community's life and influence it for Christ.

V. DUTY TO THE BROTHERHOOD

A neglected aspect of the Christian's responsibility is his neglect of his duty to those believers within the Christian fellowship—the brotherhood. The whole body of believers, who profess the same faith and share the fellowship within the church, have obligations to one another. To belong to the church is not only to be a part of the Christian brotherhood, but to belong is to share in the total Christian obligation. The Apostle Peter declared: "Honour all men. Love the brotherhood. Fear God. Honour the king."[34]

The best definition of a true church is "a fellowship." The Early Church gripped its age not only by its fresh doctrine, but with its strange and unusual fellowship. An amazed and startled world could not comprehend the Christians' love for one another. Membership carried as its essence, a sense of belonging one to another, and involved a sense of sharing. The believers were characterized by "gladness and singleness of heart."

---

[34] 1 Peter 2:17.

Christians today must have that kind of fellowship, that sense of belonging, of loving, of sharing. Fellowship in the New Testament meaning is an important part of the Church's existence. However, "fellowship" does not seem to be an adequate translation of the Greek word, *koinonia*, used to describe their togetherness. The term seems to mean a close spiritual relationship between the believers and God, but is widened to describe the spiritual uniting one with the other and indicates the common life of the community of believers. There is an evident meaning of mutual interdependence and responsibility among the believers. *Koinonia* in its fullest meaning is a comprehensive description of the unique life of the brotherhood and is fundamentally concerned with participation in things in which others also participate.[35]

Christians must show themselves before the world as true brethren. Believers are called to fellowship and to spiritual unity. Christian fellowship should produce a heart throb, a concern, a vital interest, and a sincere helpfulness among the brotherhood. All the duties of the believer to the church are also obligations to his fellow Christians. The believer's primary duty to the brotherhood is that he live an exemplary life of love and of service.[36]

A Life of Love

A soul-shaking personal experience brings the believers into one body: "So we, being many are one body in Christ, and everyone members of another."[37] Each member of the body has its function, and each function is necessary for the harmonious development of the whole. This is true of the relationship between the believer and the brotherhood. It speaks of individual obligation to the

---

[35] Robert W. Spike, *Tests of a Living Church*. (New York: Association Press, 1961), p. 15 ff.

[36] 1 Corinthians 1:9, 10.

[37] Romans 12:5. See also 1 John 4:7-21.

whole body of believers. The believer is obligated to live a life of love.

Jesus commanded: "That ye love one another, as I have loved you." He also stated that men would know His disciples because they would "have love one to another." Paul prayed for the Thessalonian believers "to increase and abound in love one toward another, and toward all men." And declared that this would establish their hearts in holiness before God.[38]

Inner Character of the Life. The best way to analyze the nature of brotherly love is to observe it in action. There are certain characteristics that should be expressed in a life of love toward the brotherhood. The believer's action toward his brethren should express the nature of his spiritual life.

1. *Sincerity.* The Christian must live a blameless life of holiness before the brethren. There should always be transparent honesty in all his relations. There can be no pretense or imitation. The spiritual life among the brethren must come from within with the external actions being the manifestation of this inner life. Sincerity will be expressed in an earnest desire to relate the outward conduct to the inward experience and to the spiritual attitude of the heart.

2. *Humility.* The Christian must live a life of humility toward God and man and never exalt himself above his brother. Paul made a very pertinent remark concerning humility when he exhorted every man "not to think of himself more highly than he ought to think." He commanded: "Be ye kindly affectioned one to another with brotherly love; in honor preferring one another." Paul believed that the Christian should humbly consider his brother's interests before his personal desires.[39]

---
[38] John 13:34, 35; 1 Thessalonians 3:12.
[39] Romans 12:3, 10.

Pride is the parent of gross sins and the spirit of pride causes bitter factions in the body of believers. The Christian must be conscious that he is a mere recipient of the grace of God and that all men stand equal before God. The believer must never take pride in his own knowledge or strength, because the sufficiency for the Christian life is always in God.[40]

3. *Faithfulness.* The Christian owes it to his fellow believers to be faithful. He must stand steadfast and unmovable in the faith. The believer must be firm in his stand for the truth and uphold the New Testament standard of conduct with all diligence. This steadfastness will give his life balance and will gender confidence among the brethren.[41]

4. *Spiritual Growth.* The believer must not only stand firm and defend the faith, but he must grow and mature and enjoy spiritual progress. By nature of his Christian experience, the believer possesses many virtues, but there is always room for progress. Each believer is obligated to the brotherhood to "grow in grace and knowledge."[42]

5. *Kindness.* There must be a friendly atmosphere of good will present in the brotherhood. The Christian must have the welfare of all believers at heart. There must never be any bitterness or ill will allowed among the believers. Note these words in Ephesians: "Let all bitterness, and wrath, and anger, and clamour, and evil speaking, be put away from you, with all malice: And be ye kind one to another, tenderhearted, forgiving one another, even as God for Christ's sake hath forgiven you."[43]

The inner nature of the Christian life is such that the

---
[40] 2 Corinthians 3:5.
[41] 1 Corinthians 15:58.
[42] 2 Peter 2:18; Colossians 1:9-11.
[43] Ephesians 4:31, 32; 2 Corinthians 2:7, 8.

believer desires and works for the spiritual and material welfare of the brotherhood.

Outward Manifestations of the Life. The life of love among the brethren will express itself in Christian conduct that reveals its inner character. The fellowship will be an "active love" that manifests itself in word and deed. All the believer's conduct will be "rooted and grounded in love.["44]

Within the group life of the church, the Holy Spirit constantly brings every member to confront the absolute holiness of Jesus Christ. All must walk with a contrite heart, accepting forgiveness from the same God whose holiness judges them. Certain standards of discipleship are agreed upon within the brotherhood, and no member passes private judgmental opinion upon another. The entire body of believers seeks to maintain purity of faith, holiness of life, and unity of fellowship by redemptive discipline.

To accomplish this, each believer must "walk in love" and avoid everything that could be harmful to his brother. He should always speak "the truth in love" and express the truth in all his life among the brotherhood. In an effort to maintain order and mutual understanding, the Christian ought to bear with his brother and make allowance for his actions. By love, the believers should "serve one another." An active concern for the spiritual welfare of the believers must be demonstrated. The agreement in the brotherhood must always be: "Let us therefore follow after the things which make for peace, and the things wherewith one may edify another." Spiritual care for the brotherhood is only part of brotherly love. It is also expressed in mutual co-operation and helpfulness in all of life.[45]

---

[44] Ephesians 3:16-21.
[45] Ephesians 4:2, 15; Galatians 5:13; Romans 14:19.

An Example in Life and Service

The powerful discipline of a pure life within the brotherhood constantly searches out sin in the group. When a member of the brotherhood breaks ranks by unchristian conduct, the entire group suffers and mourns. The erring one is made aware of his condition by the spiritual example of the fellowship. He is called, with compassion, to repent and to reunite his life with the living fellowship. With love and tenderness, those who are spiritual lead the erring soul back to an active fellowship with God and his fellow men.[46]

The Christian fellowship carries with it certain responsibilities. Decisions about conduct must be made not only in the light of the believer's relationship to God, but also in regard to his relationship to the brotherhood. A Christian must always remember that others are watching his example. He may have to forego something he considers harmless for the sake of his Christian example. The believer's reason for abstaining from various "questionable" activities does not rest upon a legalistic argument, but rather his abstinence is dependent upon his love for Jesus Christ and his concern for his brethren.

Consider the conscience of a weaker brother. There are many areas of life where a mature Christian may not see basic harm; however, his participation in these areas may cause a weak brother to stumble. A Christian must be careful not to offend those who follow his example. A good illustration of this situation can be found in Paul's first letter to the Corinthians.[47] To the Corinthian saints who trusted in the true God the many idols of the city and the consequent sacrifices meant nothing. Some felt that since they did not recognize the idol gods that it would be permissible to eat the meat

---
[46] Galatians 6:1.
[47] 1 Corinthians 8:1-13.

sold in the market that had been dedicated to the idols. However, Paul seemed to say that the stronger Christian must not eat the meat because the weaker brother would not fully understand the whole matter. The believer must never become a stumbling block to the weak of the brotherhood.

No individual believer can come to the fullness of the statue of Christ by himself. It takes the whole Christian brotherhood working together to achieve such perfection. However, each believer must make his contribution to the edifying of the brotherhood. The contribution can best be made by living a life of love and by being an example in service. The believer must ask himself whether or not his Christian example challenges others to live more consecrated lives and if the way in which he maintains his Christian faith makes him a better member of the brotherhood.

VI. DUTY TO ONE'S NEIGHBOR

The primary concern of the believer is for the brotherhood; however, he must maintain a proper attitude toward the world outside the brotherhood. The idea of universal benevolence is clearly expressed in Galatians: "As we have therefore opportunity, let us do good unto all men, especially unto them who are of the household of faith." Paul says: "Follow that which is good, both among yourselves, and to all men." The Christian must manifest a spirit of forbearance and kindness toward all men, because the coming of Christ is near. The believer must always seek the best interest of his neighbor.[48]

Christian love is a strong force in man's social life and should have first place on any list of social virtues. "Love worketh no ill to his neighbour: therefore love is the fulfilling of the law." Concerning the virtues of

---
48 Galatians 6:10; 1 Thessalonians 5:15; Philippians 4:5.

faith, hope, and love, Paul stated: "The greatest of these is love." The life of love manifested toward the brotherhood will also be evident in the Christian's relations with all men. He is commanded to love his neighbor with the same love he has for himself and the brotherhood. This is a vital part of the believer's Christian witness.[49]

The meaning of "neighbor" has been much discussed. In Leviticus the term is used to regulate the relations within the nation of Israel. The Old Testament meaning of neighbor was of value in uniting Israel and preventing their exposure to the moral and spiritual evils found outside the covenant. However, the New Testament meaning of "neighbor" is much wider. It is evident that Jesus, in His teaching concerning the neighbor, referred to more than just personal friends, relatives, or fellow citizens. He included even the enemy.

One of the greatest commands of all time is this: "Thou shalt love thy neighbor as thyself."[50] The duty to one's neighbor is closely related to the individual's duty to himself. (See Duty to Self p. 71.) A man must first consider himself. This is a basic requirement of the plan of God. When man has fulfilled his obligations to himself and to his God, he will not neglect his responsibility as a Christian neighbor.

The parable of the Good Samaritan teaches that every person in need is a neighbor regardless of race, station, or creed, and that every man who aids another displays the neighborly spirit. Not only are those who live next door, or in the same community considered to be the Christian's neighbor, but all men in the world who are in any kind of need are neighbors. The needy person does not have to belong to the believer's church, be a citizen of his country, or of the same race to be considered a neighbor. A basic need is the only requirement. Even the heathen are neighbors of the Christian com-

---
[49] Romans 13:10; 1 Corinthians 13:13.
[50] Matthew 22:39.

munity, and each individual believer has a spiritual obligation to them. Such as the Christian possesses, mentally, physically, and socially, he must share with those in need. By doing so, he will be a good neighbor.[51]

VII. DUTY TO ONE'S ENEMY

The Christian must believe that love is stronger than hate and must never compromise his obedience to Christ's command: "Love your enemies."[52] The believer must decide once and for all that discipleship means absolute obedience to Jesus Christ. He cannot beat a comfortable retreat back to Old Testament ethics which condoned something less than redeeming Christian love of the enemy.

"Love your enemies" is not counsel of perfection for select saints. It is a general law of the Kingdom; it is a precept of that exceeding righteousness that Jesus Christ requires of all who follow Him. The law of retaliation was repealed by Jesus. He is our example. Jesus Christ taught nonresistance by precept and by example. However, His application of this truth was personal and did not include the defense of others. A believer can defend the faith, protect his family and his own life, but he must never retaliate or seek revenge for personal reasons.

Can a man love his enemies and do good to them that despitefully use him? Many persons regard this as an extremely difficult duty, and others think it is impossible. Certainly it is unnatural to love an enemy, because to do so is spiritual work. Yet, the believer is commanded to love his enemies. It is the spirit of Christ who prayed: "Father, forgive them, for they know not what they do" that motivates such love. An understand-

---
[51] Luke 10:25-37.
[52] Matthew 5:43, 44.

ing that it is not the man himself but sin that causes wrong conduct creates a desire to pray earnestly that the enemy will be delivered from the ways of sin and will be brought into fellowship with God and man.[53]

Patient and calm endurance of the wrongdoer is a Christian characteristic. Christian love is demonstrated by loving the unloveable. However, loving an enemy does not mean that the wrong is condoned or that the evil conduct is approved. The Christian regards his enemy with the love of compassion and sympathy, and he is willing to forgive him in an effort to win him to Jesus Christ. Indeed, life is too short to permit any part of it to be spent in holding a grudge, seeking revenge, or showing an evil spirit. Such a situation always depresses the mind and robs life of its joys, while a forgiving spirit gives joy, peace and a satisfaction to all of life. It should be remembered that meakness is not weakness. A kindly and gracious spirit toward all men is entirely consistent with constructive living. Treating men as Jesus treated them is not a demonstration of weakness, but it is a manifestation of the meekness and tenderness of Jesus Christ.

Loving one's enemies is another instance where Christian righteousness is to exceed the scribes and the Pharisees. The Christian must maintain a positive, helpful, and prayerful attitude to fulfill his obligation to his enemy.

1. *Positive.* The Christian must have a positive attitude toward his enemy. There must be more than just patience. Loving an enemy is not to forbid a wrong course of action but to make it a positive duty. The Christian must seek ways to express his love to his enemy.

2. *Helpful.* An attitude of helpfulness will logically follow a positive desire to love. Love must be expressed

---

53 Luke 23:34; Romans 7:20.

or it dies. It must flow out in deeds and works of kindness. Mere negative nonresistance is not sufficient. This is clearly stated in Romans:

> Recompense to no man evil for evil. Provide things honest in the sight of all men. If it be possible, as much as lieth in you, live peaceably with all men. Dearly beloved, avenge not yourselves, but rather give place unto [God's] wrath: . . . for in so doing thou shalt heap coals of fire on his head. Be not overcome of evil, but overcome evil with good.[54]

Evil must be overcome by positive action and by good works humbly done. The enemy is conquered when Christian love destroys his hostility and proves the Christian to be his friend.

3. *Prayerful.* Patience or nonresistance is supported by love and love is sustained by prayer. Loving an enemy can be effective and can be sustained by sincerely praying for the enemy. When a Christian is wrongly used or his personal relationship has been strained because of ill will, the believer must pray for God to change the heart of the evildoer. In the meantime, the Christian must continue to demonstrate the positive virtues of love, mercy, and forgiveness as taught by Jesus Christ.

It is true that the enemy is not justified in mistreating the believer, but he will have to give account to God. The Christian duty is to love, to pray for, and to deal honestly and justly with all men regardless of their action or personal attitude toward the Christian. However, there are some people with whom it seems impossible to get along for any period of time. Paul's counsel should be remembered: "If it be possible, as much as lieth in you, live peaceably with all men." In such cases,

---
[54] Romans 12:17-21.

after all efforts to effect a change in the enemy's attitude and life have failed, he should be left alone.[55]

The Christian must be certain that this "leaving the enemy alone" is not the result of personal indifference. Such an enemy should head the believer's "prayer list." An enemy that is not changed by prayer and love must still be loved and dealt with justly. Justice is not inconsistent with love, but rather it gives strength and dignity to it. There is no exception—the disciple of Jesus Christ must love his enemies.

VIII. DUTY TO THE SINNER

Discipleship speaks of separation from old ties and an exclusive adherence to Jesus Christ. The line has been clearly drawn between the old and the new life, between the saint and the sinner. This raises the question of the relationship between the Christian and the sinner.

A basic desire of believers who have experienced the joy of a genuine Christian consecration is to persuade others to enter into the same experience. This is a spiritual expression of the natural impulse to share any enjoyable experience with others. The primary purpose of the believer's consecration is found in his attitude toward the sinner. The compelling missionary attitude of believers is expressed in these words of an unknown poet:

> Can we whose souls are lighted
> With wisdom from on high;
> Can we to souls benighted
> The lamp of life deny?

Christians must be a "light to the lost" and point men to the Saviour. The church that practices love will be best able to evangelize. Converts will be attracted to the Christian faith when believers "walk in wisdom toward

---
[55] 2 Thessalonians 3:14, 15.

them that are without." Each individual Christian must keep himself pure and "void of offense" if he is to contribute to the evangelistic outreach of the church.[56]

A Christian tends to reject those who deviate from his standard of living. The more consecrated the believer and the deeper his convictions concerning holiness of heart and life the more vigorous the rejection. Christians who are commited to Christ and take their standard of discipleship seriously must be aware of "this tendency to reject."[57] Discipleship does not afford the Christian a point of vantage from which to attack others; the believer must come to the sinner with an unconditional offer of Christian love, understanding, and fellowship.

The Christian life is more than merely believing. The believer must live Christ before his associates as a winning witness of grace. Christian life is the whole and Christian living the part. This life is a life of grace. All men stand equal before God: saved by grace through faith. It is easily understood that men will react differently to others when the main purpose for living among them is to honor Jesus Christ and to win them by His love.

Being a Christian does not endow a man with standards of judgment or special rights and privileges above his fellow man. Rather, it obligates him to others in a unique way. How easy it would be for the Christian to adopt a superior attitude and to pass unqualified condemnation on the rest of the world. This is why Jesus made it so clear that such misunderstandings would imperil discipleship. Christians are not to judge others. If they do, they will be judged by God as hypocrites themselves, and will jeopardize their Christian fellowship.[58]

Judging others blinds the believer to his own needs. When a Christian makes judgments of his own, he sets

---
56 Colossians 4:5, 6; Acts 24:16.
57 Cook, *op. cit.*, p. 12.
58 Matthew 7:1-12.

up standards of good and bad. The standard of holiness is to be applied to the believers in Christ and not to the sinner. The holiness of God and the Christian example of the believers will condemn and judge the sinner. The sinner will actually judge himself when he is brought face to face with a consecrated Christian. The Christian's source of good is God and exist only as the believer is related to God; therefore, he can never use his own goodness as a standard by which he judges others.

The Christian, as a disciple of Jesus Christ, has a new standard of conduct. This standard, however, is the result of the believer's relationship with Christ and not the cause of this relationship; therefore, the Christian has no right to judge the sinner by his standard of living. The true believer does not see his own righteousness. He sees the righteousness of Jesus Christ and constantly evaluates himself by this standard. The Christian seeks to bring his sinner friends, by precept and example, into a saving knowledge of Jesus Christ, knowing that this is the only way to cause conduct to conform to Christian standards.

Certainly there is a great gulf fixed between the Christian and the sinner, but it is well for the saint to remember that Jesus was a "friend of sinners."[59] There can be no true partnership, harmony, or agreement between the believer and the sinner, because they have nothing in common.[60] However, the Christian, being as a sinner saved by grace, can well understand the sinner's state of affairs and assist him in finding relief from the burden of sin. It is not a standard of right living that separates the Christian and the sinner; it is Christ who stands between them. The Christian must meet the sinner as prospect for the Kingdom. The Gospel should

---

59 Matthew 11:19.
60 2 Corinthians 6:14-18.

never be forced upon an unwilling heart, but the believer has an obligation to the sinner to demonstrate the reality of the Christian experience and to encourage him to seek God. The Christian must follow Paul's example who became "all things to all men" in his effort to save some.

The sinner cannot be viewed with detachment, because he has a claim on the Christian's love and service. Christians must seek to "make desciples" of their sinner friends. The believer must fervently intercede for the sinner's salvation, invite and encourage the sinner to seek forgiveness, and instruct the sinner in the basic steps to salvation from the Word of God. By loving unconditionally, the Christian can effect a condemnation of sin. Once the sinner is aware of his sins and understands the steps to salvation, the Christian can lead him into a saving knowledge of Jesus Christ. The Christian disciple does not have any special privilege or power of his own in this relationship with the sinner. The relationship is regulated by his fellowship with Jesus Christ. The simple rule of thumb that Jesus gave his disciples is clear: "All things whatsoever ye would that men should do to you, do ye even so to them."[61] When this simple rule is followed, the Christian forfeits all advantage over other men and seeks to bring all men into a fellowship with God.

IX. DUTY TO THE STATE

What is required of a disciple of Jesus Christ in his relations with civil governments? Through the years, men of the Christian faith have faced the problems of life and have arrived at certain conclusions concerning the Christian's obligation in all areas of life. In the realm of the state, the basic attitude seems to be that each

---
[61] Matthew 7:12.

believer should develop a Christian conscience and he should be determined to apply the Christian way of life to his citizenship.[62]

Christianity does not release the believer from the necessity of obedience to the civil government. The Christian lives under the protection of the state, and he is subject to all the ordinances that exist for the furtherance of social harmony and orderly living. This is to be done "for the Lord's sake." The Christian has an obligation to pray for the leaders of the state that they might be saved. The Christian and the state have no great difficulty unless the laws of the state violate the Christian's conscience.[63]

Christian Conscience

A Christian conscience is acquired by sharing the fellowship and the activity of Christian people and developing a deep concern for the Christian ideals. The Christian conscience, like man's social conscience, can be educated; therefore, the Christian is obligated to cultivate this awareness of the Christian ideals and to make an application of them to his conduct and attitude toward the state. The Christian must assume definite responsibility for maintaining Christian ideals within the state. In this age when public policy is determined by popular opinion, the importance of a Christian conscience is obvious. The Christian must not only be concerned with the subject of "Church and State," but he must be vitally concerned with the everyday issues that affect man's freedom and his way of life.

What if conscience and the state conflict? The Christian must stand on the group he believes to be holy and be willing to pay the price for his stand. Peter and John are good examples: "Whether it be right in the

---

[62] Romans 13:1, 2.
[63] 1 Peter 2:13-17; 1 Timothy 2:1-4.

sight of God to hearken unto you more than unto God, judge ye. For we cannot but speak the things which we have seen and heard."[64] T. B. Maston adequately expresses the Christian position:

> The Christian position is that all of the individual's life is to be integrated or unified around his love for Christ and his devotion to Christ's cause. The source of final authority for him is not the state . . . but what he interprets to be the will of God for his life. The insistence of the Christian conscience has been expressed by Isaac Watts as follows:
>
> Let Caesar's due be ever paid:
> To Caesar and his throne;
> But consciences and souls were made
> To be the Lord's alone.[65]

Christian Citizenship

The democratic way of life has a definite relation to the Christian faith. It has been called "an off-shoot of the Christian movement."[66] The Christian has an obligation to maintain this way of life and to apply Christian principles to public affairs.

The Christian has a responsibility to participate in the orderly affairs of state. The believer must always be Christian in this participation and will be held accountable for his action or for his indifference. The Christian can never stop with the normal standard of civic

---

[64] Acts 4:19, 20.

[65] T. B. Maston, *The Christian in the Modern World.* (Nashville: Convention Press, 1952), p. 98. Used by permission.

[66] Charles A. Ellwood, *The World's Need of Christ.* (New York: Abingdon-Cokesbury, 1940), p. 170.

responsibility; he is responsible for maintaining a life on the highest level. The Christian standard of living must be evident in all his activity. The Christian's warm personality, his sincere and inherent love of people, should be coupled with his desire to serve in a Christian application of his citizenship responsibilities. He must have the courage to express Christian convictions and a quality of firmness to stand by decisions he believes to be right and just.

The Christian citizen should never evade his obligations to the government that protects his family and which provides a land of peace in which to live and to worship according to a free conscience. All citizens must equally share the burdens of maintaining a state worthy of God's blessings. The words of Jesus are clear: "Render therefore unto Caesar the things which are Caesar's; and unto God the things that are God's."[67]

X. DUTY TO THE WORLD

The grace of God that brought salvation taught man to deny ungodliness and worldly lusts and to "live soberly, righteously, and godly, in this present world." It is obvious that the Christian is a citizen of two worlds. Jesus prayed: "I pray not that thou shouldest take them out of the world, but that thou shouldest keep them from the evil." The Christian must live in God's created world and sustain his life by the material things, but it is clear that the Christian is a citizen of heaven.[68]

The Created World of God

The world belongs to God, its Creator. Satan is called "the god of this world," but he has limited power. He

---
[67] Matthew 22:21.
[68] Titus 2:11, 12; John 17:14-16.

is not the creator or ruler of the world. Man is a part of the created world of God. The fact that a man believes in Jesus Christ and trusts Him for salvation does not change this fact. Believers are "in the world," but they are not "of the world." Paul says that "all things" including "the world," belong to those who have learned the truth of God and glory in Jesus Christ.[69]

The created world is not in itself unclean. Sin is a personal matter and does not reside in things. The world is evil only as a fallen world. The world is under the "curse of sin," but this is directly related to the sin of man. "The earth is the Lord's and the fullness thereof." All that God has made is good and may be used to sustain life and to provide joy for the creation.[70]

The Material World of Man

The material world of "things" may be hostile to the Christian life. "The world" has become a symbol of man's separation from God and "the flesh" stands as a symbol of the unredeemed man. These are destined for destruction by the judgment of God. The attitude of the Christian to the world must necessarily be one of extreme caution. Christians must resolutely separate themselves from everything that would defile them. The fight against "this world" is not entirely, or even primarily, an external matter; it is a struggle within. Notice these words of John:

> Love not the world, neither the things that are in the world. If any man love the world, the love of the Father is not in him. For all that is in the world, the lust of the flesh, and the lust of the eyes, and the pride of life, is not of the Father, but is of the world. And the world passeth away, and the lust thereof;

---
[69] 1 Corinthians 3:21, 22.
[70] Romans 14:14; Psalms 24:1; 35:5.

but he that doeth the will of God abideth forever.[71]

The world that man must not love is "this world." It will pass away. The Christian really belongs to the eternal kingdom of God built on the Word. He is at liberty to make use of the material world as God's gifts and to enjoy the created world of God, but these things must always be secondary and passing.

Christians are to use the material world for the advancement of the Kingdom. The material possessions are to be recognized as gifts of God.[72] The fact that each believer is to give to God's cause "as he hath prospered" is evidence that God is not opposed to prosperity, provided it is used for the advancement of the Kingdom. Believers are to work in the world to provide for their household and the less fortunate.[73] The material world must never become the center of existence. It may be used and even enjoyed, but it must always remain secondary to the believer's devotion and concern for the Kingdom.

The Christian should enjoy life and living, but should cultivate an attitude of detachment from the world and maintain his personal dependence on Jesus Christ. This world is not his home; the Christian is just passing through. The believer's citizenship is in heaven.

DISCUSSION GUIDE

1. What is man's primary duty?
2. What are the logical consequences of recognizing God as the Eternal Father?
3. Why was "duty to self" placed second in this book?

---

[71] 1 John 2:15-17.
[72] 2 Corinthians 9:6, 7.
[73] 1 Thessalonians 4:10-12; 2 Thessalonians 3:8-13.

DECALOGUE OF DUTY

4. Discuss the believer's self-development. Why the order: mental, physical, spiritual, and social.
5. What is the role of the church in Christian marriage?
6. Discuss the problems involved in marriage when only one is a Christian. Apply the triangle relationship to this situation.
7. How are the church and the home related? How can they co-operate for mutual beliefs?
8. Why should believers join the church?
9. What are the believer's obligations to the church?
10. How can membership be kept meaningful?
11. Discuss the church as "a fellowship."
12. What are the characteristics expressed in a life of love toward the brotherhood?
13. Discuss the meaning of "neighbor."
14. What attitudes must the Christian maintain to fulfill his obligation to love his enemy?
15. Should Christians judge others? What are the results of judging others?
16. Discuss the tendency to reject people who deviate from your standard of living.
17. What should be the believer's basic attitude toward the state?
18. What must the Christian do if conscience and the state conflict?
19. Why should the Christian cultivate a detachment from the material world?

BIBLIOGRAPHY

Barnette, Henlee H., *Introducing Christian Ethics*. Nashville: Broadman Press, 1961.

Bornkamm, Gunther, *Jesus of Nazareth*. New York: Harper and Brothers, translation of the 1959 edition.

Cochran, Leonard H., *Man at His Best*. New York: Abingdon Press, 1957.

Cook, Robert A., *Steps to Maturity*. Wheaton: Scripture Press Foundation, 1960.

Copi, Irving M., *Introduction to Logic*. New York: The MacMillian Company, 1953.

Eavy, C. B., *Principles of Christian Ethics*. Grand Rapids: Zondervan Publishing House, 1958.

Ellwood, Charles A., *The World's Need of Christ*. New York: Abingdon-Cokesbury, 1940.

Harrison, Everett F., Geoffrey W. Bromomite, and Carl F. H. Henry, *Baker's Dictionary of Theology*. Grand Rapids: Baker Book House, 1960.

Keyser, Leander S., *A System of General Ethics*. Burlington, Iowa: The Luthern Literary Board, 1954.

King, Geoffrey R., *Truth for Our Time*. Grand Rapids: Wm. B. Eerdmans Publishing Company, 1957.

Knudson, Albert C., *The Principles of Christian Ethics*. New York: Abingdon-Cokesbury Press, 1943.

Maston, T. B., *The Christian in the Modern World*. Nashville: Convention Press, 1952.

Meyer, F. B., *The Sermon on the Mount*. Grand Rapids: Baker Book House, 1959.

Miller, Paul M., *Group Dynamics in Evangelism*. Scottdale, Pennsylvania: Herald Press, 1958.

Oldham, J. H., *Life Is Commitment*. New York: Association Press, 1959, abridgment edition.

Oldham, Dale, *Living Close to God*. Anderson, Indiana: The Warner Press, 1957.

Spence, H. D. M. and Joseph S. Exeli, *The Pulpit Commentary*. Grand Rapids: Wm. B. Eerdmans Publishing Company, 1950.

Spike, Robert W., *Tests of a Living Church*. New York: Association Press, 1961.

Stevenson, Herbert F. (ed.), *Keswick's Authentic Voice*. Grand Rapids: Zondervan Publishing House, 1959.

Tenny, Merrill C., *New Testament Survey*. Grand Rapids: Wm. B. Eerdmans Publishing Company, 1960.

White, Reginald E. O., *The Stranger of Galilee*. Grand Rapids: Wm. B. Eerdmans Publishing Company, 1960.

Yates, J. Clyde, *Our Marching Orders in Evangelism*. New York: The American Press, 1957.